Free Speech in Contention

Elizabeth-Jane Peatfield

Free Speech in Contention

An Interdisciplinary Approach

palgrave
macmillan

Elizabeth-Jane Peatfield
Department of Criminal Justice
Liverpool John Moores University
Liverpool, Merseyside, UK

ISBN 978-3-031-94108-5 ISBN 978-3-031-94109-2 (eBook)
https://doi.org/10.1007/978-3-031-94109-2

This Palgrave Macmillan imprint is published by the registered company Springer Nature Switzerland AG
The registered company address is: Gewerbestrasse 11, 6330 Cham, Switzerland

Preface—The Importance of Free Speech

Introduction

Free speech. It's a phrase we hear all the time, but what does it really mean? And why does it matter so much? At its heart, free speech is about empowering people—giving them the chance to debate, question authority, and fight for their rights. These individual rights, when stitched together, form the fabric of society. But free speech isn't just a political tool. It's also the foundation for scientific breakthroughs, academic discovery, and cultural creativity. It's the spark that allows ideas to be tested, challenged, and sometimes completely transformed. Dr. Elizabeth-Jane Peatfield a former night club bouncer and now senior lecturer in Criminal Justice will discuss this.

This book is about that spark. It dives into why free speech is so important and where it's currently facing challenges. We'll explore the tension between free expression and hate speech, unpack the tricky question of when (if ever) the state should step in, and look at how free speech is both a tool for progress and a battleground for modern controversies. From heated debates over J.K. Rowling's comments on transgender rights to the political spin and outright lies, this book uses real-world examples to shine a light on the power—and the perils—of free speech.

As a writer and academic, the preservation of free speech is deeply personal to me. It is not just a philosophical or societal ideal but a vital part of how I approach my work. Writing and research are acts of exploration—an opportunity to question, challenge, and push boundaries.

Without free speech, the ability to question the status quo or propose latest ideas is severely limited. This freedom is the bedrock of my career and the careers of countless others in creative and intellectual fields. It is through open discourse that we learn, innovate, and inspire.

Alexander Meiklejohn, one of the great minds to study free speech, once said it's not just a right; it's a tool for self-government. In a democracy, people need access to information. They need to be able to share opinions and challenge authority without fear of censorship. Without that freedom, governments aren't held accountable, and voters can't make informed decisions. But here's the tricky part: what happens when free speech spreads lies? What if the information people rely on isn't true? Does free speech still work as it should, or does it start to tear at the very fabric of democracy it's supposed to protect?

Free speech also plays a huge role in encouraging participation. It's the key to ensuring everyone—especially marginalised communities—has a voice in shaping society. As Perry (1983) pointed out, freedom of expression is like a safety valve against tyranny. It's what allows people to stand up against unjust laws and challenge those in power. But again, the question looms: where do we draw the line? If someone's "free speech" is spreading harmful misinformation or inciting hatred, is it still protected? These are not easy questions, and as Wermiel (2018) highlights, the boundaries of free speech are always up for debate.

Now let's shift gears a little. Free speech isn't just a political tool; it's the lifeblood of progress in science and academia. Think about how science works—it's all about asking tough questions, challenging assumptions, and testing theories. Without the freedom to express ideas (even the really unpopular ones), innovation stops slowly. Oster (2013) reminds us that freedom in media and academia fuels this process by allowing ideas to spread and evolve. And then there's the "marketplace of ideas," a concept that dates back to John Milton and John Stuart Mill. It's simple: when diverse perspectives compete, the best ideas usually win.

But here's the catch: free speech in academia is under strain. Matsuda (2018) talks about how certain types of speech—especially those that are harmful or discriminatory—can make academic spaces hostile. Balancing free expression with the need to create inclusive environments isn't easy, and it's one of the biggest challenges facing universities today.

As someone who works in academia, I see first-hand how vital free speech is to education and research. It's what allows me and my colleagues to tackle difficult subjects, engage with controversial ideas, and teach students to think critically about the world around them. Without it, the academic world becomes stagnant—a place where fear of offending stifles innovation and limits learning. Yet, I also recognise the responsibility that comes with free speech. It must be used thoughtfully, with an awareness of the potential for harm, especially in diverse and inclusive settings.

Culture, too, thrives on free speech. It's what allows creators to push boundaries, share new perspectives, and reflect the world around them. Whether it's literature, music, or cinema, free speech drives the innovation that keeps culture alive. In multicultural societies, it's even more important, because it helps diverse groups connect and understand each other. But again, as Matsuda (2018) points out, the challenge lies in making sure all voices are heard—not just the loudest ones.

So, What's Going Wrong?

If free speech is so important, why is it under threat? For starters, there's cultural censorship. Legal restrictions and societal pressures—like the rise of "cancel culture"—have sparked fiery debates about what can and can't be said. Then there's the media, which should be a champion of free speech but is grappling with its own problems. Consolidation of ownership and the spread of misinformation have made it harder for people to trust what they read or watch. And social media? It's both a blessing and a curse. On the one hand, platforms like Twitter/X and Facebook have democratised communication. On the other, they've become hotbeds for hate speech, fake news, and polarisation.

Take the "trans debate" as an example. When J.K. Rowling shared her views on gender and sex, it unleashed a storm of reactions—from fierce defenders of her right to speak out to equally passionate critics who said her words were harmful. Then there's Brexit, a political event shaped by free speech, for better or worse. The referendum was filled with bold claims—some accurate, many not—that shaped how people voted. These examples show how free speech can ignite debate, but they also reveal the potential for harm when it's misused or weaponised.

Hate speech is one of the thorniest issues here. Matsuda (2018) argues that speech that harms or dehumanises others, like racism, erodes social cohesion and equality. While protecting free speech is essential, we also need to think about the cost—who's hurt by certain kinds of speech, and what can we do to protect them?

Why This Book Matters

This book will take a deep dive into these questions. Is free speech truly indispensable for democracy, progress, and cultural growth? Can it empower people to make informed decisions, spark scientific discovery, and enrich our collective understanding? Or are its challenges—misinformation, hate speech, polarisation—too great to ignore?

At the heart of this book is the argument that free speech isn't just an abstract ideal or a lofty philosophical concept. It's a practical, everyday necessity. It's what keeps democracies vibrant, societies inclusive, and innovation alive. But it's not without its challenges. Protecting and promoting free speech means constantly navigating its limits, grappling with its misuse, and ensuring it remains a force for progress and understanding.

For me, as both a writer and an academic, free speech is a deeply personal issue. It underpins the work I do, the stories I tell, and the ideas I share. I believe in its transformative power to challenge norms, spark dialogue, and drive change. In academia, free speech is not just about the right to express an opinion but the responsibility to engage critically with opposing views. It is about fostering an environment where difficult conversations can happen, and where perspectives that may be uncomfortable or unpopular are examined rather than silenced.

Debate and discussion are fundamental to both research and teaching. A university should be a place where differing opinions are not just tolerated but encouraged, where students and scholars alike can challenge, refine, and reshape their ideas. A commitment to free speech does not mean an absence of boundaries—there is a duty to ensure that discourse remains respectful and constructive. But within those boundaries, there must be room for rigorous debate, intellectual risk-taking, and, most importantly, a safe space where individuals can express their views without fear of being shut down.

Through critical engagement with contemporary debates, this book seeks to illuminate the path forward. Free speech, when meaningfully protected and practiced, strengthens democracy, fosters social progress, and allows us to confront uncomfortable truths rather than shy away from them.

Free speech is worth fighting for—but only if we're willing to face its complexities head-on.

Liverpool, UK

Elizabeth-Jane Peatfield

The original version of the book has been revised. A correction to this book can be found at https://doi.org/10.1007/978-3-031-94109-2_11

Acknowledgement

This book would not have been written without the prework that has been done by some of the proponents of free speech such as Toby Young of the FSU to Professor Joe Phoenix who has stood for free speech no matter the challenges to herself. This is a book built on the bravery of others who put their heads above the parapet and for them I am truly grateful. I would also like to thank my university Liverpool John Moores University and my colleagues in Criminal Justice for supporting free speech and rejecting cancel culture to allow for challenging and sometimes uncomfortable topics to be debated free from threats. Debate and discussion are paramount in any academic setting, and we cannot just support free speech that is in line with our own positions.

I was brought up in a house of strong, working-class women who were not backwards in coming forward, if they thought something was wrong. Free speech has always been important in my family so thank you my long-suffering husband Russ, as well as Sandra, Pam, John, Sapphire and Leah who must put up with me shouting at the TV, arguing with myself when writing and talking incessantly to them about free speech. It's written now guys so you are off the hook till the next one.

Thank you for always supporting this bolchie opinionated scouser.

Contents

CHAPTER 1

What Do We Mean by Free Speech

Abstract This chapter interrogates the multifaceted concept of free speech, establishing it not only as a legal right but as a vital instrument for democracy, social progress, and intellectual inquiry. It critically examines the contested nature of free speech across cultural, political, and institutional domains, highlighting the tension between its preservation and its limitations. Through the lenses of radicalisation, academia, and the media, the chapter explores how free speech can both safeguard open dialogue and inadvertently perpetuate harm. The chapter engages with UK legal frameworks—particularly the Human Rights Act 1998 and the Public Order Act 1986—to illuminate the boundaries of lawful expression and the state's role in regulating hate speech and offensive conduct. It contends that while free speech is foundational to a democratic society, it is not absolute; rather, it must be continually negotiated against competing rights and social imperatives. Ultimately, the chapter advocates for a nuanced, balanced approach that respects the freedoms of expression while ensuring protection from incitement, discrimination, and harm.

Keywords **Free Speech**—The right to express opinions without government restriction · **Democracy**—A system of government where citizens have power through elected representatives and public debate · **Marketplace of Ideas**—A concept suggesting that free, open discourse leads to the discovery of truth · **Censorship**—the suppression or

E.-J. Peatfield, *Free Speech in Contention*,
https://doi.org/10.1007/978-3-031-94109-2_1

prohibition of speech considered objectionable or harmful · **Liberalism**—A political ideology emphasising individual rights, freedoms, and limited government interference · **Harm Principle**—John Stuart Mill's idea that speech should only be restricted to prevent harm to others · **Pluralism**—A condition where multiple groups, beliefs, or opinions coexist and are respected in society · **Tolerance**—Acceptance of differing views, beliefs, or identities

The Complexities and Necessities of Free Speech

At the outset of this discussion, it is crucial to establish a shared understanding of what free speech truly entails. The concept of free speech is often met with significant disagreement across cultural, academic, and political spheres, leading to varied interpretations of its meaning. At its core, free speech represents the right to express ideas and opinions without fear of censorship or retaliation. However, this principle is far from universally agreed upon in practice. Societies grapple with questions of its limits, such as whether restrictions on speech constitute an infringement on individual rights or whether such boundaries are necessary to protect others from harm. Who determines these rules, how they are enacted, and the variations in their enforcement across contexts add layers of complexity to the issue.

Free speech is more than a legal principle; it is a foundational pillar of democracy and societal progress. It provides the framework for open dialogue, enabling individuals to discuss, debate, and challenge ideas. In doing so, it fosters critical thinking, innovation, and the peaceful resolution of disputes. However, the contemporary landscape of free speech is increasingly fraught with tensions, particularly in contexts where it intersects with sensitive social issues such as radicalisation, the role of academia, and the responsibilities of the media.

One of the most compelling arguments for the preservation and promotion of free speech lies in its role as a tool to combat radicalism. In an era marked by growing polarisation and extremism, creating spaces for open discussion becomes imperative. Radical ideologies, whether political, religious, or social, often thrive in environments where dissent is stifled, and grievances remain unaddressed. When individuals or groups feel silenced or marginalised, they are more likely to seek out echo chambers that reinforce their beliefs, escalating the potential for radicalisation. Free speech serves as a counterbalance to this risk by allowing individuals to voice their frustrations, engage in dialogue, and confront ideas that may challenge their own perspectives. For instance, allowing open discussions on controversial topics provides opportunities to debunk misinformation, present counterarguments, and foster understanding between opposing viewpoints. Suppressing speech, on the other hand, risks driving dissent underground, where it becomes more difficult to monitor and address.

In the context of countering radicalism, free speech is particularly vital in identifying and addressing the root causes of extremist ideologies. Programs aimed at deradicalisation often rely on dialogue and education to challenge the narratives that fuel radical beliefs. By creating environments where these narratives can be openly discussed and scrutinised, societies can encourage individuals to reconsider and ultimately reject harmful ideologies. However, this requires a delicate balance, as unchecked free speech can also be weaponised to spread hate speech or incite violence. As argued by Benesch (2014), suppressing speech can exacerbate radicalisation by driving extremist narratives underground, making them harder to counter. Therefore, the challenge lies in crafting policies that protect free expression while mitigating its potential to cause harm.

Academia has long been regarded as a bastion of free speech, where scholars and students alike are encouraged to explore ideas, question established norms, and contribute to the advancement of knowledge. The principle of academic freedom is rooted in the belief that intellectual progress depends on the ability to pursue truth without fear of censorship or reprisal. However, recent years have witnessed growing concerns about the erosion of free speech in academic settings, with debates over "cancel culture," "safe spaces," and the boundaries of acceptable discourse becoming increasingly prominent.

The need for free speech in academia cannot be overstated. According to Lukianoff and Haidt (2018), limitations on free speech in academic environments inhibit intellectual curiosity and critical thinking, both of which are essential for societal progress. Universities are not only centres of learning but also arenas for robust debate and the exchange of diverse perspectives. Restricting speech in these settings undermines the very purpose of higher education, which is to equip individuals with the critical thinking skills necessary to navigate complex social, political, and ethical issues. When students and faculty are discouraged from expressing unpopular or controversial opinions, the academic community as a whole suffers from intellectual stagnation. Moreover, free speech in academia plays a crucial role in fostering social progress. Many of history's most significant movements for change, from civil rights to environmental justice, have been catalysed by the challenging of prevailing orthodoxies within academic institutions. By protecting the right to question and dissent, universities serve as incubators for ideas that have the potential to transform society. Schmid (2013) highlights that creating safe spaces for open dialogue encourages individuals to critically evaluate extremist ideologies, fostering resilience against radicalisation for example.

However, the push for free speech in academia must also grapple with the need to create inclusive environments that respect the dignity of all individuals. Matsuda (2018) argues, speech that perpetuates discrimination or marginalisation can create hostile environments that inhibit learning and participation for marginalised groups. The challenge lies in striking a balance between promoting open dialogue and preventing speech that marginalises or harms vulnerable populations. This requires universities to establish clear guidelines that uphold free expression while addressing its potential to perpetuate inequality or discrimination.

The media is another critical arena where free speech plays a pivotal role. As the "fourth estate," the media serves as a watchdog, holding those in power accountable and providing the public with the information necessary to make informed decisions. Free speech is the lifeblood of journalism, enabling reporters to investigate and report on issues of public interest without fear of censorship or retaliation. However, the media's role in promoting free speech extends beyond its function as a disseminator of information. It also serves as a platform for diverse voices and perspectives, fostering dialogue and debate on a wide range of issues. In doing so, it helps to create a more informed and engaged citizenry, which is essential for the functioning of a healthy democracy.

Despite its importance, the media's ability to uphold free speech is increasingly under threat. Around the world, journalists face censorship, harassment, and violence for their reporting, while media outlets contend with economic pressures and the rise of misinformation. As suggested by Ward (2014), press freedom is essential for ensuring transparency and accountability in democratic societies. Without it, corruption and authoritarianism can flourish unchecked. These challenges underscore the need to protect press freedom as a cornerstone of free speech. At the same time, the media must also navigate the ethical responsibilities that come with its role as a purveyor of information. While free speech allows for the expression of a wide range of viewpoints, it also comes with the responsibility to ensure accuracy, fairness, and respect for the dignity of individuals and communities. Striking this balance is particularly critical in an age of digital media, where the rapid dissemination of information can amplify both the benefits and risks of free speech.

The debates surrounding free speech often hinge on the question of where to draw the line between permissible and impermissible speech. While the principle of free speech is enshrined in many legal systems, its implementation is rarely absolute. Most societies impose restrictions on speech that incites violence, promotes hate, or endangers public safety. However, determining what constitutes harmful speech and who gets to make that determination remains a contentious issue.

One of the key challenges in regulating free speech is the potential for abuse. Laws designed to curb harmful speech can be weaponised to suppress dissent, particularly in authoritarian regimes. Even in democratic societies, the enforcement of speech restrictions can disproportionately impact marginalised groups, further entrenching existing inequalities. This underscores the importance of ensuring that any limitations on free speech are narrowly defined, transparent, and subject to robust oversight.

Free speech is a fundamental right that underpins the functioning of democratic societies, the advancement of knowledge, and the promotion of social progress. Its role as a tool against radicalism, a cornerstone of academic inquiry, and a pillar of journalistic integrity highlights its multifaceted importance. However, the exercise of free speech is not without challenges, particularly in contexts where it intersects with issues of harm, inequality, and power dynamics. Striking the right balance between protecting free expression and addressing its potential risks requires ongoing dialogue, vigilance, and a commitment to the principles of justice and inclusivity. With this in mind we have to be aware of what are the rights to free speech and what are the limitations?

Free Speech and Legal Protections

Free Speech and the Human Rights Act 1998: Incorporating Article 10 of the European Convention on Human Rights

The first piece of legislations to consider is the Human Rights Act 1998 (HRA) which incorporates into UK law the rights enshrined in the European Convention on Human Rights (ECHR), including the fundamental right to freedom of expression under Article 10. This provision plays a pivotal role in protecting free speech while balancing its exercise with the rights of others and the interests of society at large. Article 10 of the ECHR outlines the right to freedom of expression in two parts. The first establishes the right itself, stating: "Everyone has the right to freedom of expression. This right shall include freedom to hold opinions and to receive and impart information and ideas without interference by public authority and regardless of frontiers."

The second part qualifies this right, acknowledging that it is not absolute. Limitations may be imposed if they are "prescribed by law" and "necessary in a democratic society" for specific purposes, including national security, public safety, prevention of disorder or crime, protection of health or morals, protection of the reputation or rights of others, preventing the disclosure of information received in confidence, maintaining the authority, and impartiality of the judiciary.

This dual structure reflects the need to balance individual freedoms with broader societal interests, ensuring that freedom of expression is exercised responsibly and without infringing on the rights of others. By incorporating Article 10 into domestic law, the HRA ensures that UK citizens can directly invoke their right to freedom of expression in domestic courts. Public authorities, including government bodies, local councils, and law enforcement agencies, are legally obligated to respect and protect this right. Courts must also interpret legislation in a manner consistent with Article 10 wherever possible. The HRA provides individuals with a powerful tool to challenge restrictions on their speech. For example, journalists can invoke Article 10 to defend their right to publish investigative reports, activists can rely on it to protect their right to protest, and artists may use it to safeguard creative expression.

Limitations and Balancing Tests

Despite its fundamental importance, freedom of expression is not an unlimited right. The HRA allows for restrictions, provided they meet a strict legal test. Any limitation must be:

Prescribed by Law: The restriction must be clearly defined in law, ensuring that individuals understand what is prohibited. Necessary in a Democratic Society: The restriction must address a pressing social need and be proportionate to the aim pursued. Pursuant to Legitimate Aims: The restriction must align with one or more of the legitimate aims specified in Article 10(2). This balancing act ensures that freedom of expression is not used to incite hatred, promote violence, or harm the reputation or safety of others.

The incorporation of Article 10 under the HRA has been particularly significant in areas such as media freedom, political speech, and public demonstrations. Journalists have relied on Article 10 to resist gag orders and protect confidential sources, while campaigners and protestors have invoked it to defend their right to peaceful assembly and advocacy. However, challenges remain, especially in balancing this right with concerns about hate speech, misinformation, and privacy. Courts must weigh the competing interests of free expression and societal harm, often making nuanced judgements that shape the boundaries of the right. The incorporation of Article 10 of the ECHR into UK law through the Human Rights Act 1998 affirms the centrality of freedom of expression in a democratic society. While the right is subject to limitations, its protection under the HRA ensures that individuals can challenge restrictions and hold public authorities accountable, reinforcing the principles of democracy, accountability, and human dignity.

The Public Order Act 1986

The next key piece of legislation to consider it is the Public Order Act 1986. The Public Order Act 1986 is a key piece of legislation in the UK that seeks to balance the fundamental right to free speech with the need to protect individuals and communities from harm, particularly in the form of incitement to hatred. Enacted to address public disorder, this legislation has evolved to include provisions targeting hate speech and behaviours that threaten public safety, aiming to strike a balance between preserving freedom of expression and safeguarding societal cohesion.

However, freedom of speech is a cornerstone of democratic societies, enshrined in the UK under the Human Rights Act 1998 through Article 10 of the European Convention on Human Rights (ECHR). Fenwick and Phillipson (2006) argue that Article 10 provides a robust safeguard for individuals to hold opinions and communicate ideas, even if those ideas are unpopular, controversial, or offensive. This protection is foundational to democratic discourse but remains carefully qualified to ensure public order and the rights of others.

However, this right is not absolute and may be restricted to prevent harm, including incitement to hatred based on race, religion, or sexual orientation. The Public Order Act 1986 plays a critical role in defining the boundaries of lawful expression, ensuring that speech does not escalate into conduct that undermines the rights or safety of others.

The Act contains several sections relevant to incitement to hatred:

Part III of the Act specifically targets behaviours and expressions likely to incite racial hatred. It criminalises the use of threatening, abusive, or insulting words or materials, including publications, performances, and public speeches, if they are intended to stir up racial hatred or are likely to do so. For example, distributing racist propaganda or delivering speeches that promote violence against a racial group fall within this provision. However, the law requires intent or a demonstrable likelihood of incitement, ensuring that casual or unintentional speech is not unduly penalised.

(As an ex-magistrate I can tell you one of the most challenging things is to prove intent or to prove incitement was deliberate).

Part IIIA: Incitement to Religious and Sexual Orientation Hatred.

Added through amendments in the Racial and Religious Hatred Act 2006 and the Criminal Justice and Immigration Act 2008, Part IIIA addresses hatred based on religion and sexual orientation. Unlike racial hatred, the provisions for religious and sexual orientation hatred explicitly require that the speech or behaviour be threatening, not merely abusive or insulting. This distinction reflects the delicate balance between protecting vulnerable groups and upholding free expression, particularly in discussions involving religion or morality.

Public Demonstrations and Disorder

Other sections of the Act regulate public assemblies and demonstrations, prohibiting behaviours likely to provoke violence or create serious public disorder. This ensures that free speech in the context of protests does not escalate into incitement or harm to others.

The Public Order Act 1986 exemplifies the UK's approach to balancing free speech with protections against harm. On the one hand, it safeguards the right to express controversial or unpopular views, recognising the importance of open debate in a democratic society. On the other hand, it imposes limits to ensure that speech does not cross the line into incitement to hatred, which can undermine public safety and the dignity of targeted groups. While the Act provides a legal framework, its application often sparks debate. Critics argue that the thresholds for criminalising speech, particularly under the provisions for religious and sexual orientation hatred, may inadvertently chill legitimate expression. For instance, individuals expressing critical views on religious practices or policies affecting LGBTQ + rights may fear prosecution, even if their intent is not to incite hatred. Conversely, advocates for stronger protections highlight the persistent harm caused by hate speech and the need for robust enforcement. Hate crimes and incidents linked to extremist rhetoric demonstrate the potential for speech to incite violence or marginalise vulnerable groups, necessitating legal safeguards.

The Public Order Act 1986 serves as a critical mechanism for managing the tension between free speech and protections against incitement to hatred in the UK. By criminalising specific forms of harmful expression while maintaining high thresholds for intent and likelihood, the Act reflects the importance of both individual freedoms and societal safeguards. However, as societal norms and technologies evolve, the Act continues to be tested in its ability to balance these competing interests, ensuring that the principles of democracy and human dignity remain at the forefront.

Definition and Boundaries of Hate Speech Under UK Law

Balancing Free Speech and Protection

The Public Order Act 1986 exemplifies the UK's approach to balancing free speech with protections against harm. On the one hand, it safeguards the right to express controversial or unpopular views, recognising the importance of open debate in a democratic society. On the other hand, it imposes limits to ensure that speech does not cross the line into incitement to hatred, which can undermine public safety and the dignity of targeted groups. While the Acts provide a legal framework, their application often sparks debate. Critics argue that the thresholds for criminalising speech, particularly under the provisions for religious and sexual orientation hatred, may inadvertently chill legitimate expression. For instance, individuals expressing critical views on religious practices or policies affecting LGBTQ + rights may fear prosecution, even if their intent is not to incite hatred. Conversely, advocates for stronger protections highlight the persistent harm caused by hate speech and the need for robust enforcement. Hate crimes and incidents linked to extremist rhetoric demonstrate the potential for speech to incite violence or marginalise vulnerable groups, necessitating legal safeguards.

The Public Order Act 1986 and the ECHRA serve as critical mechanisms for managing the tension between free speech and protections against incitement to hatred in the UK. By criminalising specific forms of harmful expression while maintaining high thresholds for intent and likelihood, the Act reflects the importance of both individual freedoms and societal safeguards. However, as societal norms and technologies evolve, the Act continues to be tested in its ability to balance these competing interests, ensuring that the principles of democracy and human dignity remain at the forefront.

Defining and Establishing the Boundaries of Hate Speech Under UK Law

Hate speech remains one of the most contentious areas of legal and societal discourse in the UK. It is a term used to describe speech, writing, or behaviour that incites hatred or violence against individuals or groups based on certain characteristics such as race, religion, sexual orientation, or disability. While the UK strongly upholds freedom of expression as a fundamental right, it also recognises that unrestricted speech can cause harm, undermine societal harmony, and infringe upon the rights of others. Consequently, hate speech laws aim to strike a balance between protecting free speech and safeguarding individuals and communities from harm.

UK law does not provide a singular, overarching definition of hate speech. Instead, it is defined and regulated through various legal provisions that focus on incitement to hatred and the protection of individuals from harassment, alarm, or distress caused by hate-motivated conduct. Key statutes include:

Balancing Free Speech and Hate Speech Regulation

The UK's legal framework reflects an ongoing effort to balance the right to freedom of expression with the need to prevent harm caused by hate speech. The principle is rooted in Article 10 of the European Convention on Human Rights (ECHR), incorporated into UK law through the Human Rights Act 1998. Article 10 guarantees the right to freedom of expression but allows for restrictions when necessary to protect public safety, prevent crime, or safeguard the rights of others.

This balance is particularly evident in the thresholds set for hate speech offences. For example: Intent and Likelihood of Harm: In cases involving racial hatred, speech or conduct is criminalised if it is intended to stir up hatred or is likely to have that effect. For religious or sexual orientation hatred, intent is a necessary element, ensuring that the law does not penalise inadvertent or careless speech. Exemptions for Free Expression: The law explicitly protects free speech in certain contexts. For example, the provisions on religious hatred include exemptions for criticism or ridicule of religious beliefs and practices, recognising the importance of open debate in a pluralistic society.

Challenges in Defining and Policing Hate Speech

Despite these legal safeguards, defining and enforcing the boundaries of hate speech remains a challenge. Key issues include:

Subjectivity and Context: Determining what constitutes hate speech often depends on context and perception. Words or behaviours deemed hateful by some may be considered harmless or merely provocative by others, creating ambiguity in enforcement. Digital and social media: The rise of online platforms has amplified the reach of hate speech, making it more difficult to monitor and regulate. Social media companies face pressure to remove harmful content while preserving free speech, but their policies are inconsistent and lack transparency. Cultural and Political Sensitivities: Hate speech laws must navigate complex cultural and political landscapes. For instance, debates about gender identity, immigration, and religion often involve deeply held beliefs that can be difficult to reconcile with the need to prevent harm.

Establishing Boundaries: Practical and Legal Considerations

To address these challenges, the UK's legal framework incorporates several mechanisms to define and enforce the boundaries of hate speech: High Thresholds for Criminalization: By requiring intent or likelihood of harm, the law ensures that only serious cases of hate speech are prosecuted, preserving space for controversial or offensive speech that does not incite hatred. Judicial Oversight: Courts play a critical role in interpreting and applying hate speech laws, balancing competing rights and interests on a case-by-case basis. Education and Awareness: Promoting understanding of the law and the harmful impact of hate speech is essential for encouraging responsible speech and reducing reliance on criminal sanctions.

Defining and establishing the boundaries of hate speech under UK law involves balancing the right to freedom of expression with the need to protect individuals and communities from harm. The legal framework, centred on the Public Order Act 1986 and related statutes, provides clear but nuanced guidance, emphasising intent and harm while preserving robust debate and criticism. However, the dynamic nature of communication, particularly online, means that these boundaries are continually tested, requiring vigilant oversight and ongoing adaptation to uphold both free speech and societal cohesion.

Controversies Surrounding What Constitutes "Offensive" Speech

The concept of "offensive" speech is one of the most contentious aspects of legal and societal discourse in the UK. While the right to freedom of expression is protected under the Human Rights Act 1998, certain forms of speech, such as those deemed harmful or inciting hatred, are restricted. However, the line between speech that is offensive but permissible and speech that warrants legal sanction is often blurred, leading to significant controversy.

The Subjectivity of "Offensiveness"

One of the core challenges in defining offensive speech is its inherent subjectivity. What one person finds offensive, another might consider a legitimate expression of opinion or humour. This subjectivity makes it difficult to create clear legal definitions or consistent enforcement practices. For example, satire or parody can be perceived as offensive by some but celebrated as a vital form of critique by others. Similarly, cultural and generational differences further complicate consensus on what crosses the line into offensiveness.

In cases involving comedy, art, or political speech, offensiveness is particularly contentious. High-profile examples, such as controversial statements by public figures or offensive jokes on social media, often spark public outcry and legal scrutiny. These incidents illustrate the tension between protecting individuals from harm and upholding the right to challenge societal norms through provocative speech. UK law reflects this tension by regulating offensive speech primarily through statutes such as the Public Order Act 1986, the Communications Act 2003, and the Malicious Communications Act 1988. These laws prohibit speech or behaviour that is threatening, abusive, or grossly offensive, particularly when it incites hatred or causes harm.

For example, Sect. 127 of the Communications Act 2003 criminalises the use of a public electronic communications network to send messages that are "grossly offensive or of an indecent, obscene or menacing character." This provision has been widely applied to online content, leading to prosecutions for offensive tweets, posts, and messages. However, critics argue that the broad and vague wording of "grossly offensive" risks chilling legitimate expression, particularly in debates over controversial or polarised issues.

Several high-profile cases have highlighted the complexities of determining what constitutes offensive speech which we will discuss in detail later. In one case, a man was convicted under the Communications Act for posting a video on YouTube in which he trained his dog to perform a Nazi salute as a "joke." While the court deemed the video grossly offensive, the case sparked widespread debate about the limits of humour and the application of hate speech laws. Similarly, protests involving offensive language or imagery, such as those targeting LGBTQ+ pride events or religious gatherings, have raised questions about the boundaries of lawful expression. These incidents often pit the rights of protesters against the rights of those they offend, forcing courts and lawmakers to navigate the competing interests of free speech and protection from harm.

Context and intent play a crucial role in determining whether offensive speech is legally actionable. Courts often consider whether the speech was intended to cause harm, incite hatred, or provoke violence, as opposed to merely expressing a controversial or unpopular opinion (see Fino, 2024). This distinction is vital for preserving robust debate and preventing overreach in the enforcement of speech restrictions. However, the reliance on context and intent also introduces ambiguity. For instance, statements made in jest or as part of artistic expression can be misinterpreted, leading to disputes over whether they warrant legal or social consequences. The evolving nature of societal norms adds another layer of complexity. Speech that was considered acceptable in the past may now be viewed as deeply offensive, particularly in relation to race, gender, and sexuality. Movements like #MeToo and Black Lives Matter have amplified calls to hold individuals and institutions accountable for offensive speech, leading to broader discussions about the role of cancel culture and public accountability.

Conclusion

Free speech, as explored in this chapter, is a cornerstone of democratic societies, intellectual progress, and social cohesion. However, its application is far from straightforward, as it operates at the intersection of competing values, societal norms, and legal frameworks. Understanding what free speech means—and where its limits lie—requires navigating the complex balance between protecting individual rights and safeguarding public interests.

At its core, free speech embodies the right to express opinions, ideas, and beliefs without fear of censorship or retaliation. This right is essential for fostering dialogue, challenging entrenched power structures, and promoting social progress. Historically, free speech has served as a tool for advocating change, from civil rights movements to environmental justice campaigns. However, as this chapter has demonstrated, free speech is not an absolute right; it is shaped by legal, cultural, and contextual factors that determine when and how it may be restricted.

In examining the role of free speech in countering radicalism, the chapter highlighted its potential to address grievances, debunk misinformation, and foster understanding. Open dialogue can prevent radical ideologies from festering in echo chambers, offering a platform for individuals to voice frustrations and engage with differing perspectives. Yet, as scholars like Benesch (2014) argue, unchecked free speech can also be weaponised to incite hatred or violence. The challenge lies in crafting policies that balance the promotion of free expression with measures to mitigate harm.

In academia, free speech is indispensable for intellectual growth and innovation. Universities have long been bastions of free inquiry, where challenging established norms and exploring controversial ideas are integral to their mission. However, debates over cancel culture, safe spaces, and the limits of acceptable discourse underscore the tensions within academic environments. While free speech is vital for fostering critical thinking and societal progress, it must be reconciled with the need to create inclusive spaces that respect the dignity of all participants. As Matsuda (2018) and Lukianoff and Haidt (2018) suggest, this balance requires nuanced approaches that uphold both academic freedom and inclusivity.

The media, another critical domain of free speech, plays a dual role as a watchdog and a platform for diverse voices. In democratic societies, press freedom is essential for ensuring transparency, holding power to account, and providing the public with the information needed to make informed decisions. However, the rise of misinformation, economic pressures on journalism, and attacks on media freedom pose significant challenges. As Ward (2014) notes, safeguarding free speech in the media requires not only legal protections but also ethical accountability to ensure accurate, fair, and respectful reporting.

The chapter also addressed the legal frameworks that govern free speech in the UK, particularly through the Human Rights Act 1998 and the Public Order Act 1986. These laws reflect the need to balance individual freedoms with broader societal interests, such as preventing incitement to hatred or protecting public safety. However, the enforcement of these laws often sparks controversy, particularly in cases involving hate speech or offensive expression. Determining the boundaries of free speech is a dynamic and context-dependent process, shaped by evolving societal norms and competing interpretations of harm.

Ultimately, free speech is both a right and a responsibility. It empowers individuals to participate in democratic processes, challenge injustice, and contribute to societal progress. At the same time, it requires thoughtful stewardship to ensure that it does not perpetuate harm or exacerbate inequalities. Striking the right balance between protecting free expression and addressing its potential risks demands ongoing dialogue, robust legal frameworks, and a commitment to inclusivity and justice. By embracing these principles, societies can navigate the complexities of free speech while preserving its foundational role in democracy and human dignity.

Questions to Reflect On

1. Where should society draw the line between protecting free speech and preventing harm?
   - Consider legal, ethical, and cultural perspectives.
2. How can free speech both challenge and reinforce power structures in institutions like universities and the media?
   - Reflect on examples where speech has driven change versus where it has caused exclusion or harm.
3. In what ways might limiting offensive or radical speech unintentionally contribute to greater polarisation or extremism?
   - Think about the consequences of suppression versus engagement.

Bibliography

Benesch, S. 2014. *Dangerous Speech: A Proposal for Countering Online Hate Speech*. Washington, DC: World Policy Institute.

Fenwick, H., and G. Phillipson. 2006. *Media Freedom Under the Human Rights Act*. Oxford: Oxford University Press.

Lester, A., D. Pannick, and J. Herberg. 2019. *Blackstone's Guide to the Human Rights Act 1998*, 7th ed. Oxford: Oxford University Press.

Lukianoff, G., and J. Haidt. 2018. *The Coddling of the American Mind: How Good Intentions and Bad Ideas Are Setting Up a Generation for Failure*. New York: Penguin Press.

Matsuda, M. J. 2018. Words that Wound: Critical Race Theory, Assaultive Speech, and the First Amendment. *Critical Race Theory*, 2nd ed. Chicago: University of Chicago Press

Schmid, A. P. 2013. Radicalisation, De-radicalisation, Counter-radicalisation: A Conceptual Discussion and Literature Review. *ICCT Research Paper* 1 (1): 1–39.

Ward, S. 2014. *Ethics and the Media: An Introduction*. Cambridge: Cambridge University Press.

CHAPTER 2

Censorship, Cancel Culture, and Free Speech

Abstract This chapter explores the rise of cancel culture and its implications for free speech, academic freedom, and digital discourse. It examines how cancel culture functions both as a tool of social accountability—particularly for marginalised communities—and as a potential threat to intellectual openness and due process. Through contemporary case studies involving public figures, media controversies, and landmark legal decisions such as Jo Phoenix v. The Open University, the chapter interrogates the tension between holding individuals accountable and preserving space for disagreement, redemption, and intellectual freedom. It assesses the impact of cancel culture on academia, highlighting concerns around self-censorship, the erosion of debate, and the influence of ideological conformity. The chapter also addresses the regulation of online speech, focusing on the role of Big Tech and emerging legislation such as the UK's Online Safety Bill. By critically engaging with digital platforms' power over content moderation, the protection of vulnerable groups, and the ethical challenges of algorithmic censorship, the chapter argues for a balanced, transparent, and rights-respecting approach to managing speech in the digital age. Ultimately, it positions cancel culture as a contested arena in which democratic values, social justice, and freedom of expression must be continually renegotiated.

Keywords **Cancel Culture**—Social or professional backlash against individuals for perceived offensive or harmful speech ·

E.-J. Peatfield, *Free Speech in Contention*,
https://doi.org/10.1007/978-3-031-94109-2_2

Accountability—Holding individuals or institutions responsible for their actions or words · **De-platforming**—Preventing someone from expressing views via institutional or online platforms · **Chilling Effect**—When fear of backlash discourages individuals from expressing their opinions · **Social Media Activism**—the use of platforms like Twitter or Instagram to promote causes or challenge power · **Freedom vs. Harm**—The debate between protecting speech and protecting individuals from harmful language · **Public Shaming**—Criticising someone publicly, often online, for behaviour or statements · **Cultural Power**—The influence that norms, narratives, and media have over what is considered acceptable speech

The Rise of Cancel Culture and Its Impact on Academic and Public Discourse

This chapter delves into the rise of cancel culture, a phenomenon that has sparked intense debate and controversy in recent years. We will explore how cancel culture influences public discourse, shaping what can—and cannot—be said in the public sphere. Additionally, we will examine its implications for academia and research, where the free exchange of ideas is both a foundational principle and a potential flashpoint for conflict. By analysing the dynamics of cancel culture, this chapter aims to unpack its impact on intellectual freedom, societal progress, and the boundaries of acceptable expression.

What Exactly Is Cancel Culture?

Cancel culture refers to the collective practice of withdrawing support from individuals or organisations due to behaviours or statements deemed offensive or unacceptable. This phenomenon, particularly prevalent on social media platforms, has sparked significant debate regarding its implications for free speech and public discourse.

Proponents of cancel culture argue that it serves as a mechanism for marginalised communities to hold individuals and institutions accountable for harmful actions or rhetoric. By amplifying voices that have historically been suppressed, cancel culture can challenge systemic injustices and promote social change. For instance, online callouts have been instrumental in movements like #MeToo, where survivors of sexual harassment and assault have used digital platforms to share their experiences and demand accountability. Ng (2020) reflects on this aspect, noting that cancel culture can be seen as a form of digital media participation that empowers marginalised voices.

Conversely, critics contend that cancel culture fosters a climate of fear, discouraging open dialogue and the exchange of diverse perspectives. The potential for public shaming and professional repercussions may lead individuals to self-censor, thereby undermining the foundational democratic principle of free speech. A study by the Pew Research Centre (2021) found that while some view calling out others on social media as a means of promoting accountability, others perceive it as a form of censorship that stifles free expression.

The decentralised nature of cancel culture, lacking formal guidelines or enforcers, contributes to its unpredictability. Public opinion, often volatile and influenced by the rapid dissemination of information online, plays a crucial role in determining the outcomes of cancellation attempts. This unpredictability can result in disproportionate consequences, where individuals face severe backlash for actions or statements that may not warrant such a response. Dershowitz (2020) argues that cancel culture can undermine due process and free speech, as decisions to cancel individuals are often made without objective, fair-minded criteria.

While the practice of ostracising individuals for deviant behaviour is not new, the amplification provided by digital platforms has intensified its impact. The speed and reach of social media enable cancel culture to effect change rapidly, but also raise concerns about the potential for mob justice and the erosion of nuanced, constructive discourse. Ng (2020) discusses how digital media participation has transformed traditional forms of public shaming into more pervasive and immediate phenomena.

In summary, cancel culture embodies a complex interplay between the empowerment of marginalised voices and the potential suppression of free speech. Its decentralised and rapid nature, facilitated by digital platforms, presents both opportunities for social accountability and challenges to open dialogue. As such, it remains a contentious aspect of contemporary discourse, warranting ongoing examination and critical reflection.

Modern Examples of Cancel Culture

J.K. Rowling, the author of the *Harry Potter* series, became a central figure in debates around cancel culture after sharing opinions about transgender issues, which many interpreted as transphobic. In a 2020 essay, Rowling detailed her concerns about sex, gender, and women's rights, arguing that biological sex is a significant reality with implications for society and law (Rowling, 2020). Her statements, particularly on platforms like Twitter/ X, ignited fierce backlash from LGBTQ+ activists and allies, who viewed her comments as harmful and called for boycotts of her works. As noted by Furedi (2021), this controversy reflects broader tensions surrounding cancel culture, as public figures face intensified scrutiny and reputational consequences in digital spaces.

In response to the backlash, Rowling and other prominent writers signed an open letter in *Harper's Magazine* defending the importance of free expression, warning that the suppression of dissenting views undermines democratic discourse (Harper's Magazine, 2020). Critics of cancel culture argue that the swift, collective condemnation of Rowling's views exemplifies how such mechanisms can stifle debate and marginalise alternative perspectives. However, advocates emphasise the importance of holding influential figures accountable for perpetuating rhetoric perceived as exclusionary or harmful. This case underscores the inherent tension between accountability for public figures and the safeguarding of free expression in an increasingly polarised digital landscape.

In 2019, comedian Kevin Hart stepped down as the host of the Academy Awards after a series of past tweets and jokes resurfaced, many of which were deemed homophobic. Despite issuing apologies, Hart faced intense criticism, with some arguing that his actions reflected a pattern of discriminatory behaviour. Critics of cancel culture pointed out that these were old statements for which Hart had previously apologised, raising questions about whether society allows for growth and redemption in public life. The controversy surrounding Kevin Hart's withdrawal from hosting the Oscars exemplifies the complexities of cancel culture, particularly in relation to the potential for personal growth and societal forgiveness. As noted by Clark (2020), the incident highlights the challenges in balancing accountability for past actions with the recognition of an individual's capacity for change. This case underscores the tension between holding public figures accountable for previous misconduct and acknowledging their efforts towards personal development and redemption.

The #MeToo movement, which aims to combat sexual harassment and assault, has also intersected with cancel culture. Figures like Harvey Weinstein, Kevin Spacey, and Louis C.K. were publicly called out, resulting in professional fallout and social ostracism. While many saw these actions as long-overdue accountability, others argued that the swiftness of public condemnation, often preceding legal processes, blurred the lines between justice and trial by public opinion. This case emphasises the duality of cancel culture as both a tool for empowerment and a potential threat to due process.

In 2021, Dr. Seuss Enterprises decided to stop publishing six books that contained racially insensitive imagery. Critics of cancel culture viewed this decision as an attack on a beloved author and a form of unnecessary censorship. Supporters argued that the decision was a responsible acknowledgement of harmful stereotypes. This example illustrates how cancel culture can extend beyond individuals to cultural artefacts, sparking debates about historical context, cultural sensitivity, and the evolution of societal norms.

Comedian Dave Chappelle faced backlash for his Netflix special, The Closer, in which he made jokes about transgender individuals. Activists called for the special's removal and boycotts of Netflix, arguing that Chappelle's material was harmful and perpetuated transphobia. Others defended him, emphasising the role of comedy as a space for challenging societal norms and discussing controversial topics. This incident reignited debates about artistic freedom, the limits of humour, and whether cancel culture restricts creative expression.

Broader Implications of Cancel Culture

Cancel culture is often framed as a tool for accountability, allowing marginalised communities to challenge powerful individuals or organisations who perpetuate harm. For instance, it has amplified voices calling for justice in cases of sexual misconduct, racism, and other systemic issues. Supporters argue that cancel culture democratises accountability, enabling ordinary people to hold public figures to higher standards of conduct. However, critics contend that cancel culture can veer into censorship, silencing dissenting voices and creating a culture of fear where people are reluctant to express controversial or unpopular opinions. This concern is particularly acute in creative fields, academia, and journalism, where open debate and the free exchange of ideas are essential.

Social media platforms have played a pivotal role in the rise of cancel culture. They allow issues to gain traction quickly, often bypassing traditional gatekeepers such as the media or courts. While this democratisation of public opinion is a powerful tool, it also comes with risks, such as misinformation, mob mentality, and the inability to control the long-term consequences of online backlash. Another controversial aspect of cancel culture is its lack of a clear path for redemption. Critics argue that cancel culture often denies individuals the opportunity to learn, grow, and make amends. In many cases, the focus remains on punishment rather than reconciliation or progress, raising questions about whether it is effective as a mechanism for meaningful societal change. The controversies surrounding cancel culture highlight its dual nature as both a force for accountability and a potential threat to free expression. By examining its complexities and broader implications, it becomes clear that cancel culture is not a monolithic phenomenon but a reflection of societal tensions over power, privilege, and the evolving boundaries of acceptable discourse. Understanding these dynamics is essential for navigating its impact on public life, academia, and the creative industries.

Arguably there are four main impacts for this type of cancellation:

First is the democratisation of accountability. Cancel culture has been described as a means for marginalised groups to hold powerful figures accountable, effectively redistributing attention and recognition. This perspective emphasises the empowerment of historically oppressed communities through digital activism. **Second**, the risks of censorship and silencing as this phenomenon has also been critiqued for potentially stifling free speech and open debate, particularly within academic settings. Concerns have been raised about self-censorship among scholars who fear repercussions for expressing controversial views, which may undermine academic freedom. **Third**, the role of social media and the ability in modern time for the rapid dissemination of information on social media platforms have intensified the effects of cancel culture. While these platforms facilitate swift mobilisation for social justice causes, they also contribute to the spread of misinformation and can exacerbate polarised discourse. **Fourth** and finally, the lack of redemption pathways as cancel culture often lacks mechanisms for forgiveness or rehabilitation, focusing predominantly on punishment. This punitive approach may hinder constructive dialogue and the potential for personal growth or societal progress.

Concerns about self-censorship among scholars due to fear of repercussions for expressing controversial views have been extensively discussed in academic literature. This phenomenon is often linked to the rise of cancel culture and its impact on academic freedom. For instance, Norris (2020) explores how perceived pressures for intellectual conformity may lead to self-censorship, potentially undermining the diversity of perspectives essential for academic discourse. The role of social media in amplifying cancel culture is also significant. Ng (2020) discusses how digital platforms facilitate swift mobilisation for social justice causes but also contribute to the spread of misinformation and exacerbate polarised discourse. This dual-edged nature of social media can intensify the effects of cancel culture, influencing both public perception and individual behaviour. Furthermore, the lack of redemption pathways in cancel culture has been critiqued for focusing predominantly on punishment without offering mechanisms for forgiveness or rehabilitation. This punitive approach may hinder constructive dialogue and the potential for personal growth or societal progress. Ng (2020) reflects on how cancel culture's emphasis on public denunciation can lead to the silencing of diverse perspectives, raising concerns about its long-term implications for democratic values and social cohesion.

Accusations of Self-censorship Due to Societal Pressures

Cancel Culture in Academia: A Debate Between Myth and Reality

Cancel culture has emerged as a divisive phenomenon in academic settings, with profound implications for intellectual freedom, research, and pedagogy. In her 2023 study, Cancel Culture: Myth or Reality?, Pippa Norris investigated the prevalence and impact of cancel culture in academia, challenging popular narratives while emphasising the complexities of this issue. Norris's work highlights the tension between fostering inclusive academic environments and maintaining the free exchange of controversial or unpopular ideas. Cancel culture in academia is often portrayed as a stifling force that silences dissenting voices and discourages scholars from addressing controversial topics. This perception has fuelled debates about whether universities are abandoning their role as bastions of free thought and critical inquiry. Critics including myself have argued that fear of backlash—whether from colleagues, students, or the public—has led to self-censorship among academics, particularly those whose research or teaching touches on politically sensitive issues such as race, gender, or identity politics. This has led to the creation of agencies such as the Free Speech Union, Academics for Academic Freedom, and Students for Academic Freedom in order to safeguard staff and students from the threat of being cancelled.

Norris, however, challenges the extent of this narrative, questioning whether cancel culture is as pervasive as it is often portrayed. Drawing on empirical data, she finds that while high-profile cases of "cancellation" dominate media discourse, they represent only a fraction of academic life. Most scholars report experiencing little to no direct impact from cancel culture in their professional activities. Nevertheless, she acknowledges that even the perception of cancel culture can have a chilling effect, discouraging some academics from engaging with contentious topics. One of the key issues Norris addresses is the intersection of cancel culture and academic freedom. Universities traditionally uphold the principle of academic freedom, allowing scholars to pursue research and express ideas without fear of institutional reprisal. However, the rise of cancel culture raises questions about how this freedom interacts with evolving societal norms and expectations. For instance, scholars engaging with controversial research topics—such as the biology of gender differences or critiques of cultural practices—may face criticism that extends beyond academic debate. Norris emphasises that while constructive criticism is an essential part of scholarly discourse, cancel culture often involves ad hominem attacks, public shaming, and demands for retraction or dismissal. Such responses, even if rare, can deter academics from pursuing innovative or provocative lines of inquiry.

The legal case involving Jo Phoenix, a professor who specialises in issues of gender and justice, further illustrates the complexities surrounding cancel culture in academia. Phoenix has argued that her career was significantly damaged due to her views on gender and sex-based rights, which led to sustained hostility from colleagues and students, including formal complaints and exclusion from academic opportunities. Her legal case against the Open University, where she alleged institutional failure to protect her academic freedom and well-being, highlights how "cancellation" can extend beyond reputational damage to legal disputes over workplace discrimination and harassment.

Phoenix's case is particularly significant because it underscores the difficulty of maintaining a balance between academic freedom and the increasingly polarised landscape of identity politics. While universities have long been spaces of debate and intellectual challenge, the modern climate has made it far more difficult for scholars to engage in discussions that touch on sensitive or controversial topics. The backlash against Phoenix was not merely about disagreement with her views but rather an attempt to delegitimise her position within academia, raising serious questions about the extent to which dissenting voices are tolerated within scholarly institutions.

This case raises important questions about the responsibilities of universities in protecting scholars whose work provokes controversy and whether the boundaries between academic disagreement and professional misconduct are becoming increasingly blurred. If universities are unwilling or unable to safeguard their academics from ideological conflicts, the fundamental principles of free inquiry and open debate are at risk. The treatment of Phoenix suggests that some institutions may be prioritising ideological conformity over the foundational academic principle of contestation. When debate is stifled due to fear of backlash, academia ceases to function as a space for critical thinking and becomes instead a battleground for competing dogmas.

In a landmark ruling, Jo Phoenix won her case, with the tribunal finding that the Open University had failed in its duty to protect her from discrimination and harassment. The outcome of this case sets a significant precedent for academic freedom, reinforcing the legal obligations of universities to safeguard scholars from ideological pressure and workplace hostility. More than just a personal victory, Phoenix's case has wide-ranging implications for academic institutions across the UK and beyond, signalling that universities must take seriously their duty to protect staff from targeted campaigns that seek to undermine their professional standing.

Phoenix's victory not only underscores the tangible consequences of cancel culture but also signals a potential shift in how universities handle contentious debates within academia. If institutions fail to uphold robust protections for free expression, they risk eroding the very essence of what makes academic discourse meaningful. As higher education grapples with an era of heightened ideological division, cases like this serve as a stark reminder that academic freedom must not be contingent on prevailing social attitudes but rather upheld as an essential principle of scholarly integrity. The ruling in her favour reinforces the idea that universities must not only allow but actively defend diverse viewpoints—even those that challenge dominant narratives.

The wider impact of this case may well be felt beyond academia. In a society where free speech is increasingly contested, the verdict serves as a warning against the dangers of institutional complicity in ideological suppression. Universities, as bastions of critical thought, must resist the impulse to side with popular opinion at the expense of scholarly debate. If they fail in this duty, they risk not only legal consequences but also the broader erosion of trust in academia as a space for genuine intellectual exchange.

Generational and Cultural Divides

Norris's analysis highlights generational and cultural divides in perceptions of cancel culture within academia. Younger academics and students are more likely to advocate for inclusive and respectful discourse, sometimes interpreting controversial ideas as harmful or oppressive. Older academics, in contrast, often emphasise the importance of intellectual rigour and the willingness to challenge societal taboos. This generational tension reflects broader societal debates about the balance between free speech and protection from harm. Cultural differences also play a role. In countries with strong traditions of academic freedom, cancel culture is often framed as a threat to the core mission of universities. In contrast, in contexts where academic discourse has historically been constrained by authoritarian regimes or cultural norms, calls for greater inclusivity may be seen as part of a broader push for social justice and democratisation.

Another critical aspect of Norris's work is the relationship between cancel culture and efforts to create more inclusive academic environments. Advocates for inclusivity argue that certain forms of speech or research perpetuate systemic inequalities and harm marginalised communities. For example, some students and faculty may view discussions that question the validity of trans identities or critique affirmative action policies as not just controversial but actively harmful.

Norris acknowledges the legitimacy of these concerns but cautions against conflating harm with discomfort. She argues that discomfort is an inherent part of intellectual growth and that universities have a responsibility to foster environments where difficult conversations can take place. However, she also emphasises the need for clear institutional policies that balance the protection of academic freedom with the cultivation of respectful and inclusive campus climates.

Policy Implications and Moving Forward

Norris's study concludes by exploring the policy implications of cancel culture in academia. She advocates for greater transparency in how universities handle complaints and controversies, ensuring that decisions are guided by consistent principles rather than public pressure. She also calls for a renewed commitment to academic freedom, coupled with initiatives to promote civil discourse and mutual understanding among students and faculty. Ultimately, she argues that while cancel culture may not be as pervasive as its critics claim, its perception poses a challenge to academic life. Addressing this challenge requires a nuanced approach that acknowledges the complexities of free speech, inclusivity, and institutional responsibility. By fostering open dialogue and supporting diverse perspectives, universities can navigate the tensions of cancel culture while remaining true to their mission of advancing knowledge and understanding.

Norris's work on cancel culture in academia offers a balanced perspective, challenging alarmist narratives while recognising the real pressures facing scholars in an era of heightened cultural and political sensitivities. The phenomenon is neither entirely a myth nor an unassailable reality; instead, it reflects the evolving dynamics of academic and societal discourse. Her findings underscore the importance of protecting academic freedom while fostering an environment that encourages both rigorous debate and respect for diverse identities and experiences. The growth of organisations such as Academics for Academic Freedom or the Free Speech Union has shown that this is a subject academics are taking seriously.

Regulation of Speech on Digital Platforms and the Role of Big Tech Companies

The regulation of free speech on digital platforms has become a key focus for policymakers, advocacy groups, and tech companies alike. Efforts such as the Online Safety Bill in the UK reflect growing recognition of the need to balance free expression with protections against harmful content. Advocacy groups such as *Stop, Think, Connect* have long criticised digital platforms for their inadequate efforts to address issues such as misinformation, hate speech, and online harassment. These organisations emphasise that while digital platforms provide opportunities for open dialogue, their lack of oversight has enabled the unchecked spread of harmful, misleading, or offensive material (Bradshaw et al., 2021). Supporting this stance, a report by Global Action Plan (2020) revealed that 75% of children do not feel safe online, with 90% reporting instances of appearance-based criticism and pressure to change. This data underscores the pressing need for robust measures to protect vulnerable populations, particularly young people, from the damaging psychological effects of online harm. The rapid dissemination of harmful content can exacerbate mental health issues, increase social anxiety, and perpetuate harmful stereotypes (Livingstone et al., 2020).

Big Tech and Content Moderation

The role of Big Tech companies such as Facebook, Twitter, and YouTube in regulating digital spaces is increasingly under scrutiny. These platforms, which once positioned themselves as neutral hosts of public discourse, have become powerful gatekeepers of speech, shaping global conversations and determining what content is visible, suppressed, or removed. While they claim to support free expression, critics argue that their content moderation policies are inconsistent, opaque, and often reactive rather than proactive. In many cases, platforms enforce their policies selectively, responding to public pressure, media outrage, or shifting political winds rather than adhering to a clear and principled approach.

Gillespie (2018) highlights that platforms act as arbiters of speech, selectively enforcing policies that may align more closely with business interests than with safeguarding users. Their financial models, which prioritise user engagement and advertising revenue, often create conflicts between maintaining open discourse and removing harmful content. This raises questions about who ultimately controls the boundaries of online speech and whether private corporations should wield such significant influence over global communication. The lack of transparency in how decisions are made—particularly in cases of high-profile de-platforming—fuels concerns that these companies function as unaccountable regulators of digital expression.

Additionally, O'Neil (2016) argues that algorithmic content moderation—driven by machine learning systems—can unintentionally amplify harmful content while suppressing legitimate speech, particularly affecting marginalised communities. Algorithms often prioritise engagement, leading to the amplification of polarised, sensational, or harmful material, which increases profits at the expense of user safety. The same algorithms that detect and remove explicit hate speech may also disproportionately silence voices discussing sensitive topics such as racial justice or LGBTQ+ rights. The automated nature of moderation also means that context is frequently lost, leading to unfair or inconsistent application of platform policies.

As we have already discovered, the UK's Online Safety Bill represents a legislative attempt to address these concerns. The Bill places a legal duty on platforms to take down illegal content promptly and ensure that harmful but legal content is managed responsibly. Platforms are also required to demonstrate transparency in their moderation processes and improve protections for children and vulnerable users (Department for Digital, Culture, Media & Sport, 2021). In theory, this legislation could compel platforms to act more responsibly, preventing them from turning a blind eye to online abuse, misinformation, and exploitation.

Proponents of the Bill argue that such measures are necessary to combat hate speech, misinformation, and online harms that have flourished in poorly regulated digital spaces. They contend that Big Tech has been slow to act when it comes to protecting users from coordinated harassment campaigns, extremist content, and child exploitation, making government intervention essential. However, critics warn of potential overreach, where increased regulation could stifle free speech and limit legitimate debate (Barnett, 2022). The definition of "harmful but legal" content remains particularly contentious, as it opens the door to subjective interpretations that could be used to justify disproportionate censorship.

Balancing the regulation of harmful content with the protection of free expression is a significant challenge. While regulation seeks to create safer digital spaces, it also raises important ethical and legal questions about censorship, privacy, and corporate accountability. As Flew et al. (2019) argue, achieving this balance requires a multi-stakeholder approach involving governments, tech companies, and civil society to ensure that regulatory frameworks are both effective and proportionate. There is also a risk that governments could exploit such legislation to suppress dissent, particularly in countries with weaker democratic protections.

The regulation of speech on digital platforms highlights the evolving tension between free expression and content safety. Advocacy groups, supported by empirical evidence, stress the urgent need for oversight to address online harms, particularly for vulnerable groups like children. However, the role of Big Tech in this process—alongside legislative efforts such as the Online Safety Bill—raises critical questions about transparency, accountability, and the unintended consequences of regulation. If platforms err too far on the side of caution, they risk undermining free speech by silencing voices that challenge mainstream narratives. Conversely, if they fail to act decisively against harmful content, they contribute to an online environment where misinformation, abuse, and extremist ideologies can flourish.

As digital platforms continue to shape public discourse, striking a balance between safety and free speech will remain an ongoing challenge for policymakers and society alike. The key question is whether meaningful regulation can be achieved without compromising the democratic principles that free expression is meant to uphold. The future of digital speech regulation will likely depend on whether governments and tech companies can create mechanisms that ensure fairness, consistency, and transparency—without succumbing to political or commercial interests.

A particularly pressing concern within this debate is the protection of younger users online. Digital platforms are now an intrinsic part of childhood and adolescence, with social media, streaming services, and online gaming communities playing a central role in young people's socialisation, education, and recreation. However, these spaces, originally designed with adult users in mind, expose children to significant risks, including cyberbullying, online grooming, exposure to harmful content, and the impact of algorithm-driven engagement patterns that can promote unhealthy behaviours.

The challenge of safeguarding children online is not simply about content moderation; it is also about ensuring that digital environments are designed with child safety in mind from the outset. Critics argue that social media platforms have historically prioritised growth and engagement over user protection, leading to an environment where young people are exposed to extreme, distressing, or misleading content. The addictive design of many platforms—built to maximise screen time through infinite scrolling, autoplay, and targeted notifications—has also raised concerns about the long-term impact on mental health, particularly among teenagers.

One proposed solution to these issues has been the introduction of stricter age verification measures. The UK's Online Safety Bill includes provisions aimed at ensuring platforms implement robust age checks to prevent underage users from accessing inappropriate content. However, enforcing these measures presents significant technical and ethical challenges. Current verification systems, such as self-reported age declarations, are easy to bypass, while more rigorous approaches, like government-issued ID verification, raise concerns about user privacy and data security. Critics also warn that strict age verification could create unintended barriers for legitimate users, particularly in cases where individuals lack access to formal identification or are uncomfortable sharing personal data with large tech corporations.

Beyond age verification, the issue of parental controls and digital literacy remains crucial. Many parents struggle to keep up with the rapidly evolving digital landscape, leaving children vulnerable to online harms. While some platforms provide parental controls and safety features, these are often underutilised due to a lack of awareness or complexity in implementation. A broader approach to digital safeguarding would require a combination of regulation, platform accountability, and education initiatives that equip parents, teachers, and children with the knowledge and tools to navigate the digital world safely.

The ethical and legal complexities of regulating digital speech become even more apparent when considering how these measures intersect with broader concerns about censorship, surveillance, and corporate power. Efforts to protect children and vulnerable users must be carefully balanced to avoid excessive restrictions that limit legitimate speech. There is also the risk that governments could use child safeguarding legislation as a Trojan horse for wider internet regulation, granting authorities the power to control content in ways that extend beyond child protection.

One of the most contentious aspects of digital speech regulation is the role of algorithmic moderation in content policing. While AI-driven moderation is often presented as a solution to filtering harmful material at scale, it is far from infallible. Algorithms struggle to understand context, leading to the wrongful removal of legitimate discussions while failing to catch harmful content that evades detection through coded language or subtle imagery. This challenge is particularly acute for younger users, who may engage with niche online communities where harmful content is disguised in ways that automated systems fail to detect.

The growing push for regulation also raises concerns about the disproportionate influence of Big Tech in shaping digital governance. Many of the world's largest platforms operate across multiple jurisdictions, meaning they are subject to varying national laws and regulatory standards. This fragmentation can lead to inconsistent enforcement, where content deemed acceptable in one country is censored in another. Additionally, there is the risk that large tech companies may use compliance costs as a justification to consolidate their dominance, disadvantaging smaller platforms that lack the resources to implement extensive regulatory measures.

Policymakers must therefore consider how to craft regulations that hold platforms accountable without inadvertently stifling competition or innovation. Striking this balance requires collaboration between governments, industry leaders, academics, and civil society groups to ensure that digital regulations serve the public interest rather than reinforcing corporate monopolies or state control over online discourse.

Advocacy groups stress the urgent need for oversight to address online harms, particularly for vulnerable groups such as children and marginalised communities. However, they also warn that poorly designed regulation could have unintended consequences, including the suppression of legitimate speech, the erosion of user privacy, and the consolidation of power among a small number of tech giants. As digital platforms continue to shape public discourse, it is clear that the debate over free speech, safety, and regulation will remain at the forefront of policy discussions for years to come.

Ultimately, the future of digital speech regulation will depend on whether governments and tech companies can develop frameworks that prioritise transparency, accountability, and fairness. This includes ensuring that platforms have clear and consistent content moderation policies, implementing safeguards that genuinely protect younger users without infringing on broader civil liberties, and fostering open dialogue about the ethical implications of emerging technologies. Without careful consideration, efforts to regulate digital spaces risk becoming yet another battleground in the wider struggle between free expression, public safety, and corporate influence in the digital age.

Conclusion

The rise of cancel culture has brought profound changes to public and academic discourse, presenting both opportunities and challenges for how societies manage free expression, accountability, and inclusivity. As this chapter has explored, cancel culture operates at the intersection of empowerment and suppression, reshaping the boundaries of acceptable speech in ways that spark intense debate. It is neither wholly progressive nor entirely destructive; rather, it represents an ongoing struggle over power, influence, and social justice in the digital age.

From one perspective, cancel culture serves as a democratising force, amplifying marginalised voices and holding powerful individuals and institutions accountable for harmful rhetoric or actions. Movements such as #MeToo and Black Lives Matter demonstrate how digital platforms can mobilise collective action and challenge entrenched power structures. By providing a mechanism for historically silenced communities to demand justice and accountability, cancel culture can foster social change and disrupt systemic inequalities. This perspective aligns with scholars such as Ng (2020), who highlight the potential of digital activism to empower marginalised groups and catalyse societal progress.

However, the unregulated and often punitive nature of cancel culture raises concerns about its impact on free expression, intellectual freedom, and constructive dialogue. Critics argue that cancel culture fosters a climate of fear, where individuals self-censor to avoid public backlash or professional consequences. This fear is particularly pronounced in academia, where scholars may shy away from controversial topics or innovative research for fear of reputational damage. Norris (2020) emphasises that even the perception of cancel culture can have a chilling effect, deterring critical inquiry and undermining the diversity of perspectives essential for intellectual growth.

Cancel culture's decentralised and unpredictable nature further complicates its role in public discourse. Decisions to "cancel" individuals or organisations often occur without consistent criteria or due process, leading to disproportionate consequences and the erosion of trust in mechanisms of accountability. High-profile cases, such as those involving J.K. Rowling, Kevin Hart, or Dr. Seuss Enterprises, highlight the tension between accountability and redemption, raising questions about whether cancel culture allows for growth, reconciliation, and meaningful societal progress.

In the digital age, the role of social media as both an enabler and amplifier of cancel culture cannot be overstated. Platforms like Twitter/X, Facebook, and YouTube provide the tools for rapid mobilisation and widespread dissemination of information, bypassing traditional gatekeepers of public discourse. While this democratisation of speech has its advantages, it also brings risks, including misinformation, mob mentality, and the amplification of polarised narratives. Gillespie (2018) and O'Neil (2016) have critiqued the algorithms driving these platforms for prioritising engagement over nuance, exacerbating divisions, and intensifying the effects of cancel culture.

The increasing reliance on algorithmic moderation also raises ethical concerns. Algorithms designed to remove harmful content often operate without human oversight, leading to over-correction or under-enforcement. In some cases, legitimate discussions about sensitive topics are censored, while extremist content continues to circulate. This lack of transparency in content moderation policies, combined with the immense influence of Big Tech in shaping public discourse, highlights the urgent need for greater regulatory oversight and accountability.

The debate over free speech in digital spaces has become even more complex with legislative efforts such as the UK's Online Safety Bill. The Bill represents a significant attempt to impose legal responsibility on platforms for harmful content, requiring them to remove illegal material while ensuring that legal but potentially harmful content is managed appropriately (Department for Digital, Culture, Media & Sport, 2021). Proponents of the Bill argue that regulation is necessary to protect users from hate speech, misinformation, and exploitation. However, critics warn that increased regulation could result in overreach, restricting legitimate debate and limiting the ability of individuals to express controversial opinions.

This tension between content moderation and free speech is particularly relevant in academia, where the impact of cancel culture can be seen in disputes over academic freedom. The case of Jo Phoenix, for instance, demonstrates how ideological conflicts within universities can escalate into legal disputes, raising important questions about the duty of institutions to protect scholars from harassment while upholding their right to engage in controversial research. As universities increasingly grapple with these issues, it is clear that the balance between safeguarding individuals from harm and maintaining intellectual freedom will continue to be a point of contention.

Another critical issue that has emerged in discussions about online regulation is child safeguarding. Younger users are uniquely vulnerable to the risks of the digital world, from exposure to harmful content to online grooming and cyberbullying. Platforms originally designed for adults have been widely adopted by children and teenagers, often without sufficient safety measures in place. While some platforms offer parental controls and content filters, many children can bypass these restrictions with ease, highlighting the need for more robust regulatory frameworks.

The Online Safety Bill includes provisions for stricter age verification requirements, aiming to prevent underage users from accessing inappropriate content. However, implementing these measures presents significant technical and ethical challenges. Self-reported age verification is notoriously unreliable, while stricter identification processes raise concerns about data privacy and surveillance. There is also the risk that such measures could exclude users who lack formal identification or create new digital divides based on access to technology.

Furthermore, the addictive design of many social media platforms has raised concerns about the mental health impacts on young people. Infinite scrolling, autoplay features, and algorithmically driven content recommendations contribute to excessive screen time, reinforcing harmful behaviours and exposing children to material they might not actively seek out. Addressing these issues requires more than just content moderation—it necessitates a fundamental shift in how platforms are designed, prioritising user safety over profit-driven engagement metrics.

Perhaps the most contentious aspect of cancel culture is its lack of a clear path to redemption. The focus on punishment rather than rehabilitation risks alienating individuals who might otherwise contribute to constructive dialogue and social progress. Critics contend that cancel culture's punitive approach often prioritises public denunciation over opportunities for education, growth, and reconciliation. This dynamic underscores the need for a more balanced and restorative approach to accountability—one that emphasises both the empowerment of marginalised voices and the importance of fostering open, inclusive dialogue.

For academia, the creative industries, and society at large, navigating cancel culture requires a nuanced understanding of its dual nature. Universities, for example, must balance their commitment to academic freedom with the need to create inclusive environments that protect students and faculty from harm. Similarly, public discourse must allow for both the accountability of powerful actors and the expression of diverse perspectives, even when those perspectives challenge societal norms.

Ultimately, cancel culture reflects broader societal tensions around power, privilege, and the evolving boundaries of acceptable speech. While it offers a platform for marginalised voices and a means of addressing systemic injustices, it also poses significant challenges to free expression and the principles of constructive debate. Addressing these challenges requires thoughtful engagement, transparency, and a commitment to both accountability and dialogue.

As digital platforms continue to shape public discourse, striking a balance between safety and free speech will remain an ongoing challenge for policymakers and society alike. The key question is whether meaningful regulation can be achieved without compromising the democratic principles that free expression is meant to uphold. The future of digital speech regulation will likely depend on whether governments, tech companies, and civil society groups can create mechanisms that ensure fairness, consistency, and transparency—without succumbing to political or commercial interests.

By fostering spaces for meaningful exchange and prioritising pathways for growth and redemption, societies can navigate the complexities of cancel culture while upholding the democratic values of free expression and mutual respect. The debate over online speech, regulation, and accountability is far from settled, but what remains clear is that digital governance must evolve in a way that protects users—particularly vulnerable groups such as children—while maintaining the freedoms that underpin democratic societies.

Questions to Reflect On

1. Does cancel culture strengthen or weaken democracy—and can it do both at once?
   - Consider the roles of accountability, marginalised voices, and the potential chilling effect on open debate.
2. Where should the boundary lie between holding people accountable and allowing for growth, dialogue, and redemption?
   - Reflect on the implications for public figures, academics, and peers.

3. Should digital platforms and governments have the power to regulate online speech—and if so, how can this be done without undermining free expression?
   - Think about the balance between safety, censorship, and corporate or state control.

Bibliography

Barnett, S. 2022. Regulating Big Tech: Balancing Safety and Free Speech. *Media, Culture & Society* 44 (3): 543–559. https://doi.org/10.1177/01634437211070025.

Bradshaw, S., H. Bailey, and P. N. Howard. 2021. Digital Misinformation and Harm in the Global South. *Journal of Information Technology & Politics* 18 (2): 162–178. https://doi.org/10.1080/19331681.2021.1910018.

Clark, M. D. 2020. *Cancel Culture: Accountability or Punishment?* https://www.researchgate.net/publication/342789456_Cancel_Culture_Accountability_or_Punishment. Accessed 16 Dec 2024.

Dershowitz, A. 2020. Cancel Culture: The Latest Attack on Free Speech and Due Process

Furedi, F. 2021. *Why Borders Matter: Why Humanity Must Relearn the Art of Drawing Boundaries*. London: Routledge.

Department for Digital, Culture, Media & Sport. 2021. *Online Safety Bill: Impact Assessment*. https://www.gov.uk/government/publications/online-safety-bill. Accessed 17 June 2024.

Flew, T., F. Martin, and N. Suzor. 2019. Internet Regulation as Media Policy: Rethinking the Question of Digital Communication Platform Governance. *Journal of Digital Media Policy* 2 (1): 1–22. https://doi.org/10.1386/jdmp.2.1.1_1.

Gillespie, T. 2018. *Custodians of the Internet: Platforms, Content Moderation, and the Hidden Decisions That Shape Social Media*. New Haven: Yale University Press.

Global Action Plan. 2020. *Children's Safety Online: Report Findings*. https://globalactionplan.org.uk. Accessed 18 Dec 2024.

Harper's Magazine. 2020. A Letter on Justice and Open Debate. *Harper's Magazine*, 7 July. https://harpers.org/a-letter-on-justice-and-open-debate/. Accessed 17 June 2024.

Livingstone, S., M. Stoilova, and R. Nandagiri. 2020. Children's Data and Privacy Online: Growing up in a Digital Age. *Media Policy Brief* 23: 1–20.

Ng, E. 2020. No Grand Pronouncements Here...: Reflections on Cancel Culture and Digital Media Participation. *Television & New Media* 21 (6): 621–627.

Norris, P., 2020. Electoral integrity in the 2020 american elections (PEI-US-2020). *Electoral Integrity Project: Cambridge, MA.*
O'Neil, C. 2016. *Weapons of Math Destruction: How Big Data Increases Inequality and Threatens Democracy*. New York: Crown Publishing Group.
Pew Research Center. 2021. Americans and 'Cancel Culture: Where Some See Calls For Accountability, Others See Censorship, Punishment.
Rowling, J.K. 2020. J. K. Rowling writes About Her Reasons for Speaking out on Sex and Gender Issues. *jkrowling.com.* https://www.jkrowling.com. Accessed 17 June 2024.

CHAPTER 3

Free Speech, Politics, Protests, and Public Assembly

Abstract This chapter explores the legal and political dimensions of protest as a core component of free speech in democratic societies. Anchored in Article 11 of the European Convention on Human Rights and the UK Human Rights Act 1998, it examines the foundational right to peaceful assembly, while interrogating its limitations in practice. Through analysis of recent legislation, such as the Police, Crime, Sentencing and Courts Act 2022, and high-profile protest movements including Extinction Rebellion and Just Stop Oil, the chapter highlights growing tensions between maintaining public order and safeguarding democratic freedoms. It considers the increasing use of vague legal definitions, pre-emptive policing, and digital surveillance, and their disproportionate impacts on marginalised groups. Case law, such as Ziegler v. CPS (2021), is used to demonstrate the judiciary's role in upholding proportionality and necessity in restrictions. Ultimately, the chapter argues that while protest remains a vital mechanism for democratic participation and social change, evolving regulatory responses risk undermining this right. A robust, proportionate, and rights-based approach is necessary to ensure that the right to dissent continues to thrive within the UK's democratic framework.

Keywords **Protest**—Public demonstration or action expressing opposition to policies or injustice · **Article 11 (ECHR)**—Guarantees the right to peaceful assembly and association in European law ·

E.-J. Peatfield, *Free Speech in Contention*,
https://doi.org/10.1007/978-3-031-94109-2_3

Disruption—Acts that interfere with normal functioning, often used as a justification to limit protest · **Police, Crime, Sentencing and Courts Act 2022**—UK law expanding police powers to limit protests · **Kettling**—A controversial police tactic of containing protesters in a small area · **Civil Disobedience**—Non-violent refusal to obey laws as a form of protest · **Proportionality**—The legal requirement that limitations on protest must be appropriate and not excessive · **Judicial Oversight**—Court reviews of state action to ensure it complies with legal standards

The Legal Right to Protest: Protections, Limitations, and Contemporary Issues

The right to protest is a fundamental aspect of democratic societies, enabling individuals and groups to express dissent, advocate for change, and hold authorities accountable. This right, enshrined under Article 11 of the European Convention on Human Rights (ECHR) and protected in the UK through the Human Rights Act 1998, has deep historical and social significance. Protests have long been a catalyst for social and political transformation, from the suffragette movement and trade union demonstrations to the civil rights protests and climate action campaigns of recent years. By enabling citizens to voice concerns and challenge power structures, protests play a crucial role in shaping laws, policies, and public discourse. However, this right is not absolute; it is balanced against the rights of others, public safety, and societal order.

Recent debates underscore the tensions between this legal right and evolving legislative, political, and social responses to protest activities. Governments often grapple with striking a balance between maintaining public order and upholding democratic freedoms. The challenge lies in defining the limits of acceptable protest while avoiding undue suppression of political expression. Controversial issues such as climate activism, public health restrictions during COVID-19, and protests against racial injustice have reignited discussions about the boundaries of free speech and assembly. High-profile actions by groups like Extinction Rebellion and Just Stop Oil, often involving disruptive tactics such as road blockades, sit-ins, and defacement of public monuments, have prompted calls for stricter policing and harsher penalties. These protests have also sparked debate over whether disruptive but non-violent civil disobedience should be considered a legitimate form of protest or a public nuisance warranting criminal prosecution.

Simultaneously, measures such as the UK's Police, Crime, Sentencing and Courts Act 2022 have been criticised for potentially eroding protest rights, particularly through broader definitions of "serious disruption." Critics argue that vague legal language increases the scope for law enforcement to restrict protests pre-emptively, raising concerns about disproportionate responses and potential infringements on civil liberties. Conversely, supporters of such legislation maintain that enhanced powers are necessary to prevent protests from impeding essential services, disrupting daily life, or posing risks to public safety.

Additionally, debates around "cancel culture" and the right to protest speeches or events highlight complexities in reconciling freedom of expression with protections against hate speech and discrimination, which is something we will discuss in more detail later. The increasing polarisation of public discourse has led to questions about whether certain protests, particularly those aimed at de-platforming speakers, align with or undermine the broader principles of free speech. Some argue that protest is an essential tool for marginalised communities to challenge harmful rhetoric, while others contend that such actions contribute to a culture of censorship.

These controversies illustrate ongoing struggles to balance individual freedoms with collective societal interests. In the coming sections, we will explore how legal frameworks, historical precedents, and contemporary challenges shape the evolving landscape of protest rights, shedding light on the fundamental question: how should a democratic society define and regulate the limits of dissent?

Article 11 of the ECHR and the Right to Protest

The legal foundation for the right to protest in the UK is primarily grounded in Article 11 of the ECHR, which guarantees the right to peaceful assembly. It emphasises the importance of collective action in a democratic society, protecting peaceful protests from undue interference by the state. Article 11 recognises protests as a legitimate means for individuals and groups to express their views, voice grievances, and advocate for causes. However, Article 11 also includes provisions for limiting this right under specific circumstances:

> *No restrictions shall be placed on the exercise of these rights other than such as are prescribed by law and are necessary in a democratic society in the interests of national security or public safety, for the prevention of disorder or crime, for the protection of health or morals or for the protection of the rights and freedoms of others.*

This clause provides governments with the ability to impose restrictions on protests, as long as those restrictions are proportionate, necessary, and prescribed by law. However, what is deemed "proportionate" and "necessary" is inherently subjective, making it vulnerable to interpretation and potential abuse. For example, critics have argued that the UK's Police, Crime, Sentencing and Courts Act 2022 grants authorities excessive discretion, enabling them to label protests as "disruptive" based on ambiguous criteria. This has led to fears of overreach and a chilling effect on public dissent.

Additionally, the enforcement of restrictions is often criticised for reflecting broader societal biases, with marginalised groups disproportionately affected. For instance, racial justice movements and climate activists have frequently faced accusations of excessive policing compared to other forms of public assembly. As courts navigate the fine line between maintaining public order and upholding democratic freedoms, these debates underscore the fragility of balancing the right to protest against competing societal interests.

The Tension Between Protest and Public Order

The legal foundation for the right to protest in the UK is primarily grounded in Article 11 of the ECHR, which guarantees the right to peaceful assembly. It emphasises the importance of collective action in a democratic society, protecting peaceful protests from undue interference by the state. Article 11 recognises protests as a legitimate means for individuals and groups to express their views, voice grievances, and advocate for causes. However, Article 11 also includes provisions for limiting this right under specific circumstances, as we previously mentioned. This clause provides governments with the ability to impose restrictions on protests, as long as those restrictions are proportionate, necessary, and prescribed by law. However, what is deemed "proportionate" and "necessary" is inherently subjective, leaving it open to broad interpretation and potential abuse. Academic critiques emphasise the risk that these subjective assessments may reflect institutional or societal biases, undermining the legitimacy of state action. Della Porta and Diani (2006) highlight that excessive or uneven enforcement of protest restrictions can erode public trust in authorities, particularly if certain groups are disproportionately targeted. Similarly, Smith (2019) argues that the framing of protests as "disruptive" often prioritises state convenience over democratic principles, marginalising dissenting voices.

The subjectivity of proportionality assessments has become increasingly contentious with the passage of legislation like the Police, Crime, Sentencing and Courts Act 2022. Scholars such as Joyce and Bennett (2022) critique this Act for granting police excessive discretionary power to impose pre-emptive conditions on protests, thereby creating a chilling effect on legitimate forms of dissent. They argue that the notion of "serious disruption" used to justify intervention is too vague, allowing authorities to target protests selectively, often focusing on movements advocating for environmental or racial justice. The courts play a critical role in ensuring that these limitations do not infringe upon the core essence of the right to protest, but their effectiveness in safeguarding democratic freedoms amidst shifting political and social landscapes remains an ongoing concern.

Contemporary Issues and Challenges

In recent years, climate activism has brought the right to protest into sharp focus. Groups like Extinction Rebellion and Just Stop Oil have adopted tactics involving civil disobedience, such as blocking major roads, disrupting public transport, and staging sit-ins. These actions aim to highlight the urgency of addressing the climate crisis but have sparked significant public and political backlash due to their disruptive nature. Authorities have responded with increased restrictions, often invoking laws designed to prevent serious disruption or protect public safety. The introduction of legislation such as the Police, Crime, Sentencing and Courts Act 2022 has further intensified this debate, granting police greater powers to restrict protests deemed overly disruptive. Critics argue that such measures disproportionately restrict the right to protest and risk criminalising legitimate dissent, particularly when protests challenge entrenched political and economic systems (Joyce and Bennett, 2022). They highlight the danger of stifling the public's ability to express grievances on urgent global issues like climate change. Supporters, however, contend that these measures are necessary to maintain societal order, protect the rights of the wider community, and ensure that essential services are not disrupted. This ongoing tension underscores the complex balance between safeguarding democratic freedoms and maintaining public order in a rapidly changing world.

Policing and Use of Force

The policing of protests remains a contentious issue, particularly regarding the use of force and tactics such as "kettling" (corralling protesters into confined areas). High-profile incidents, such as the policing of the Sarah Everard vigil in 2021, have drawn criticism for heavy-handed approaches by the police that some argue undermine public trust in law enforcement. Courts have occasionally ruled in favour of protesters when policing actions were deemed disproportionate. For instance, the European Court of Human Rights (ECtHR) has previously found the UK in breach of Article 11 for excessively restricting protests, underscoring the need for balanced and measured policing.

However, the rise of digital activism has added a new layer of complexity to the right to protest. Online platforms are now integral to organising, promoting, and amplifying protests. While this has democratised activism, it has also raised concerns about surveillance, censorship, and the use of digital evidence against protesters. Recent debates about the role of social media companies in moderating protest-related content further highlight tensions between free speech, protest rights, and public safety in the digital age.

Legislative Changes and Criticism

Recent legislative developments, such as the Police, Crime, Sentencing and Courts Act 2022, have expanded police powers to impose conditions on protests. Provisions targeting protests that cause "serious disruption" or "significant impact" have been criticised by civil liberties groups for being overly broad and subjective, potentially leading to over-policing and stifling dissent. Critics, including Amnesty International and Liberty, argue that these changes risk undermining the right to protest by granting excessive discretion to authorities. Proponents, on the other hand, emphasise the need for tools to address disruptive or harmful protests, particularly in the light of escalating tactics by certain activist groups.

Despite these challenges, judicial oversight plays a crucial role in protecting the right to protest. Courts often review whether restrictions imposed by authorities meet the tests of proportionality and necessity. In several cases, courts have ruled in favour of protesters, reaffirming the importance of this democratic right.

For example:

Ziegler v. Crown Prosecution Service (2021)

The UK Supreme Court ruled that peaceful protesters blocking a road had not committed an unlawful obstruction, as their actions were a legitimate exercise of their right to protest under Article 11. This judgement underscored the importance of balancing disruption with the fundamental right to peaceful assembly. Such rulings highlight the judiciary's role in ensuring that legislative and policing actions align with human rights obligations, providing a safeguard against potential overreach.

Proportionality is a central principle in determining the legality of restrictions on protests. Authorities must demonstrate that any limitations are necessary to achieve a legitimate aim and that they do not disproportionately interfere with the right to protest. For example, imposing conditions on the location or timing of a protest may be deemed reasonable if it minimises disruption while allowing the protest to proceed. Outright bans on protests are typically subject to stricter scrutiny and are rarely upheld unless there is unambiguous evidence of imminent harm. Proportionality ensures that the right to protest remains meaningful while accommodating the rights and interests of others. The legal right to protest in the UK, protected under Article 11 of the ECHR, is a vital expression of democratic values and public engagement. However, its exercise is subject to restrictions aimed at balancing competing rights and societal interests. The Public Order Act and other legislative frameworks provide a structure for managing protests, but their implementation often raises questions about proportionality, fairness, and the role of dissent in a democratic society.

As contemporary issues such as climate activism, digital organising, and expanded police powers reshape the protest landscape, the tensions between individual rights and societal order are likely to intensify. Safeguarding the right to protest requires vigilance, robust judicial oversight, and a commitment to protecting both free expression and public order. By navigating these challenges thoughtfully, the UK can continue to uphold the principles of democracy and the importance of public participation in shaping its future.

Restrictions on Protests in Practice and Their Implications for Free Speech

While the right to protest is legally protected in the UK under Article 11 of the European Convention on Human Rights (ECHR) and domestic laws like the Public Order Act 1986, restrictions on protests in practice often raise concerns about their implications for free speech. These restrictions are intended to balance the right to protest with public safety, order, and the rights of others. However, their application can sometimes disproportionately impact the ability of individuals and groups to express dissent.

Practical Restrictions on Protests

Police Imposed Conditions under Sects. 12 and 14 of the Public Order Act 1986, the police can impose conditions on protests if they believe the event may lead to serious public disorder, damage to property, or serious disruption to the life of the community. These conditions can include limits on the time, place, or duration of a protest. In practice, such restrictions are often criticised as being too broad and subjective, leading to inconsistencies in enforcement. Outright Prohibition in extreme cases, authorities can prohibit protests altogether, particularly if they are deemed to pose a significant threat to public safety. Such measures, while rare, can stifle dissent by preventing certain causes or viewpoints from being aired. This is especially contentious when prohibitions are perceived as politically motivated.

Recent legislative changes, such as the Police, Crime, Sentencing and Courts Act 2022, have expanded police powers to address protests causing “serious disruption” or having a “significant impact” on the public. These provisions allow the police to intervene based on perceived noise levels or potential disruptions, sparking fears that peaceful demonstrations may be unfairly targeted. Critics argue that the vague language of such laws gives excessive discretion to authorities, risking overreach, and abuse. Use of Force and Dispersal Tactics has long been criticised.

Police tactics, such as "kettling" (the containment of protesters in a confined area) or the use of force, have practical implications for protests. These measures, often justified as crowd control techniques, can deter participation in protests, especially among vulnerable groups.

Digital Surveillance and Monitoring has also been increased due to the increase of activism online, which has led to increased monitoring of online platforms by authorities. While this is aimed at preventing illegal activities, such as incitement to violence, it raises concerns about privacy and the chilling effect it may have on individuals organising or promoting protests.

Implications for Free Speech

The imposition of restrictive measures on protests can have a significant chilling effect, deterring individuals from participating due to fears of arrest, fines, or physical confrontation. This deterrence is particularly impactful on marginalised groups, for whom protests are a vital means of highlighting systemic injustices. Such restrictions not only suppress dissent but also perpetuate existing power imbalances by limiting these groups' capacity to advocate for change.

The United Nations Special Rapporteur on the rights to freedom of peaceful assembly and of association has emphasised that inaction by authorities to protect the rights of marginalised groups to freely assemble can have a chilling effect on groups that would otherwise exercise this right. This underscores the importance of safeguarding assembly rights to prevent the silencing of vulnerable communities.

Moreover, the perception of over-policing or heavy-handed restrictions can erode trust in law enforcement and governmental institutions. This erosion undermines the democratic principle that dissent, and public discourse are essential components of a healthy society. When protests are heavily restricted, activists may struggle to innovate new methods of advocacy, stifling not only free speech but also broader democratic engagement.

In essence, while regulations may aim to maintain public order, overly restrictive measures can suppress essential democratic expressions, particularly among marginalised groups, thereby reinforcing existing inequalities and hindering societal progress.

Conclusion

The interplay between politics, protests, and public assembly underscores the enduring importance of the right to protest in a democratic society. Rooted in Article 11 of the European Convention on Human Rights (ECHR) and enshrined in UK law through the Human Rights Act 1998, the right to protest allows individuals and groups to express dissent, advocate for causes, and hold authorities accountable. However, as this chapter has explored, this right is not absolute. It exists within a framework of protections and limitations designed to balance individual freedoms with public safety, societal order, and the rights of others.

The contemporary protest landscape highlights significant challenges in maintaining this balance. Climate activism, racial justice movements, and responses to public health measures during COVID-19 have brought these tensions into sharp focus. Groups like Extinction Rebellion and Just Stop Oil have employed disruptive tactics to highlight pressing global issues, such as climate change, while raising broader questions about the boundaries of acceptable protest. Legislative responses, such as the Police, Crime, Sentencing and Courts Act 2022, have sought to address these disruptions but have been criticised for their vagueness and potential overreach. Critics argue that such measures risk undermining the fundamental essence of the right to protest by criminalising legitimate dissent and disproportionately affecting marginalised groups.

The subjectivity inherent in determining what is "proportionate" and "necessary" further complicates these issues. While the principles of proportionality and necessity are designed to ensure fairness, they leave room for interpretation that can reflect institutional biases. As academic critiques have noted, excessive restrictions or uneven enforcement erodes public trust in authorities and the perceived legitimacy of the state. For example, marginalised groups and movements advocating for systemic change often face disproportionate policing, reinforcing existing inequalities and limiting their capacity for meaningful advocacy.

Policing practices, such as "kettling" and the use of pre-emptive conditions, further illustrate the fine line between maintaining public order and safeguarding democratic freedoms. High-profile incidents, such as the policing of the Sarah Everard vigil, have drawn attention to the risks of heavy-handed approaches, undermining public confidence in law enforcement. Similarly, digital surveillance of protest activity raises concerns about privacy and the chilling effect on participation, particularly in an era where online platforms are integral to organising and amplifying protests. Judicial oversight plays a critical role in protecting the right to protest and ensuring that limitations imposed by authorities align with democratic principles. Cases such as *Ziegler v. Crown Prosecution Service* (2021) reaffirm the judiciary's role in balancing public order with fundamental rights. These rulings underscore the importance of robust legal safeguards in preventing overreach and ensuring that protest remains a meaningful tool for public engagement.

However, the evolving protest landscape, influenced by digital activism, escalating tactics, and increasingly restrictive legislation, highlights the fragility of this balance. Protests are a vital means for marginalised groups to draw attention to systemic injustices and for broader society to engage in democratic discourse. Overly restrictive measures not only threaten individual rights but also risk stifling innovation in advocacy and limiting the diversity of voices in public debates.

Ultimately, safeguarding the right to protest requires a commitment to upholding democratic values while addressing legitimate concerns about public safety and societal order. This involves ensuring that legal frameworks, policing practices, and judicial interventions are fair, proportionate, and inclusive. As the UK navigates contemporary challenges, the importance of vigilance and thoughtful engagement in shaping these policies cannot be overstated. By striking the right balance, the UK can reaffirm its commitment to democracy, enabling protests to remain a powerful and legitimate expression of public will in shaping its future.

Questions to Reflect On

1. To what extent should governments be allowed to limit protests in the name of public order or safety?
   - Consider how "proportionality" and "necessity" should be interpreted and applied.
2. Are disruptive protest tactics (e.g. road blockades or sit-ins) a legitimate form of democratic expression, or should they be criminalised?
   - Reflect on the role of civil disobedience in achieving social and political change.
3. How do laws and policing practices affect different groups' ability to protest—and what does this mean for equality in public discourse?

- Think about marginalised communities and whether protest rights are equally protected in practice.

Bibliography

Amnesty International. 2022. *The Right to Protest Under Threat: Crackdowns in the UK*. London: Amnesty International. https://www.amnesty.org/en/documents/eur45/5598/2022/en/. Accessed 28 Jan 2025

Barendt, E. 2005. *Freedom of Speech*, 2nd ed. Oxford: Oxford University Press.

Della Porta, D., and M. Diani. 2006. *Social Movements: An Introduction*, 2nd ed. Oxford: Blackwell Publishing.

Ewing, K. D. 2021. The Police, Crime, Sentencing and Courts Bill 2021: A Dangerous Authoritarian Turn? *Public Law* (October): 1–16.

Human Rights Act. 1998, c.42. https://www.legislation.gov.uk/ukpga/1998/42/contents. Accessed 6 Jan 2025

Joyce, P., and T. Bennett. 2022. The Police, Crime, Sentencing and Courts Act 2022: A Threat to Protest in the United Kingdom? *Policing and Society* 32 (4): 450–469.

Liberty. 2021. *Policing Protest: A Threat to Democracy?* London: Liberty. https://www.libertyhumanrights.org.uk/report/policing-protest-a-threat-to-democracy/. Accessed 29 Jan 2025.

Mead, D. 2010. *The New Law of Peaceful Protest: Rights and Regulation in the Human Rights Act Era*. Oxford: Hart Publishing.

Oliver, D. 2022. Protest and the Law: New Developments in the UK. *Legal Studies* 42 (3): 457–478. https://doi.org/10.1017/S026138752200020X.

Police, Crime, Sentencing and Courts Act. 2022. https://www.legislation.gov.uk/ukpga/2022/32/enacted. Accessed 5 Jan 2025

Simons, G. 2022. Extinction Rebellion and the Right to Protest: Disruptive Activism in a Democratic Society. *Social Movement Studies* 21 (4): 512–530. https://doi.org/10.1080/14742837.2022.2034341.

Smith, E. 2019. Legitimacy and the Policing of Protest: The Role of Discretion in Undermining Public Trust. *British Journal of Criminology* 59 (5): 1237–1255.

UN Human Rights Council. 2021. *Report of the Special Rapporteur on the rights to freedom of peaceful assembly and of association*. A/HRC/47/25. https://undocs.org/A/HRC/47/25. Accessed 29 Jan 2025.

Walker, C. 2019. Counter-terrorism, Free Speech and the Right to Protest in the UK. *European Human Rights Law Review* 1: 35–51.

CHAPTER 4

Theories of Free Speech and Contemporary Controversies

Abstract This chapter provides a critical exploration of foundational theories of free speech and their relevance to contemporary controversies. Drawing on classical liberal thought—from John Stuart Mill's "marketplace of ideas" to Meiklejohn's democratic theory and Berlin's conception of autonomy—it outlines key philosophical justifications for free expression, including the pursuit of truth, political participation, and individual freedom. The chapter then engages with the limitations of these theories in the face of modern challenges, such as identity politics, academic freedom, religious expression, and counter-terrorism policy. Case studies—including debates over gender pronouns, campus "cancel culture," and the UK's Prevent strategy—highlight the tension between protecting speech and mitigating harm in diverse and polarised societies. The impact of digital platforms and algorithmic moderation is also examined, underscoring the complexities introduced by technological change. Through this theoretical and practical analysis, the chapter lays the groundwork for a deeper examination of the evolving boundaries of free speech in a rapidly shifting global context.

Keywords **Human Rights Act 1998**—UK law incorporating the European Convention on Human Rights into domestic law · **Article 10 (ECHR)**—Protects the right to freedom of expression with lawful restrictions · **Hate Speech**—Speech that attacks or demeans a group based on identity; often restricted · **Defamation**—False statements that

E.-J. Peatfield, *Free Speech in Contention*,
https://doi.org/10.1007/978-3-031-94109-2_4

damage someone's reputation · **Legal Proportionality**—Balancing rights with public interest in legal decisions · **Public Interest**—The common good or welfare that justifies legal limits on speech · **Libel and Slander**—Written and spoken forms of defamation, respectively · **Offensive Speech**—Expression that may shock or disturb but is often legally protected unless harmful

Introduction

This chapter explores foundational theories of free speech and examines key controversies that have arisen over the last decade. It delves into the tension between the right to free expression and competing societal values, providing a theoretical grounding for the subsequent chapters. Through this exploration, the chapter introduces intersections between free speech and topics such as academic freedom, identity politics, religion, and counter-terrorism legislation, highlighting their complexities and implications in modern contexts.

Free speech has long been heralded as a cornerstone of democratic societies, with roots in the Enlightenment and philosophical defences from theorists such as John Stuart Mill. Mill's seminal work *On Liberty* (1859) posits that the marketplace of ideas—the free exchange of thoughts, opinions, and beliefs—is essential to the pursuit of truth. He argued that only through the open contestation of ideas can societies refine their understanding and progress intellectually. The marketplace metaphor became a foundational argument for free speech in liberal democracies, underscoring its role in facilitating informed public discourse and protecting dissenting voices from suppression.

However, the practical application of free speech has always been fraught with challenges. These challenges have become particularly pronounced over the last decade as social, cultural, and technological shifts have transformed the way ideas are expressed, disseminated, and contested. The rise of social media, for instance, has amplified the reach of speech but also introduced novel issues, such as the proliferation of misinformation and the dynamics of online harassment (see Wilson and Land 2020). These developments have prompted critical reflection on whether the traditional frameworks for free speech adequately address the complexities of contemporary society.

Key controversies have emerged that challenge the scope and limits of free speech. Identity politics, for example, has sparked intense debates about the intersection of expression and harm. The use of gender pronouns has become a flashpoint, with critics arguing that enforced pronoun usage infringes on individual freedom of speech, while proponents emphasise the harm caused by misgendering and the importance of fostering inclusivity (see Fiss, 2009). These debates raise broader questions about the relationship between free speech and the protection of marginalised identities, particularly in academic and public discourse.

Academic freedom, another critical intersection, has also come under scrutiny. Universities, traditionally seen as bastions of intellectual diversity and debate, have faced growing accusations of fostering "cancel culture," where controversial views are met with calls for censorship or punitive measures. This tension reflects broader societal divides over the role of free speech in challenging dominant ideologies versus perpetuating harmful rhetoric. It also underscores the need to balance open inquiry with the responsibility to create inclusive academic environments (see Fiss, 2009).

Religious expression has similarly highlighted tensions between free speech and competing values. Events such as the Charlie Hebdo attacks reignited debates about the limits of satire, particularly when it targets deeply held religious beliefs. Such controversies often pit the principle of free expression against the need for social cohesion and respect for cultural diversity. Meanwhile, counter-terrorism legislation, such as the UK's Prevent strategy, has raised concerns about the chilling effect such policies may have on speech, especially within marginalised communities.

This chapter lays the groundwork for examining these and other controversies in greater depth. By situating free speech within its historical and theoretical contexts and addressing the challenges it faces today, it provides a foundation for understanding the nuanced debates surrounding this fundamental yet contested principle. Subsequent chapters will further explore these intersections, shedding light on the evolving role of free speech in a rapidly changing world.

Foundational Theories of Free Speech

The theories of free speech traditionally revolve around four main justifications: the search for truth, democratic participation, individual autonomy, and societal tolerance (Barendt, 2005). Each rationale contributes to the broader philosophical and legal defences of free expression for example:

The Marketplace of Ideas: John Stuart Mill's seminal work *On Liberty* (1859) argued that the free exchange of ideas, even erroneous ones, was essential for truth to emerge. Mill maintained that suppressing dissent stifles intellectual progress and risks the dominance of fallacy over fact. In the modern digital age, this rationale has been challenged by phenomena such as misinformation and echo chambers, raising questions about the marketplace's capacity to self-regulate (Sunstein, 2018).

Similarly, the concept of Democratic Function argues that free speech is integral to democratic governance, enabling citizens to critique authority and engage in public discourse. Alexander Meiklejohn (1948) emphasised that the health of democracy depends on robust protections for political speech. However, debates about the line between political dissent and harmful rhetoric—particularly in the era of social media—have intensified over the last decade.

Philosophers such as Isaiah Berlin (1969) argue that free speech is facet of autonomy and self-expression and have linked free speech to personal autonomy, arguing that the ability to express one's beliefs is intrinsic to individual freedom. Contemporary identity politics, however, has raised questions about whether certain expressions undermine others' autonomy, particularly in cases of hate speech or misgendering (Butler, 1997).

Theorists like Karl Popper (1945) warned of the "paradox of tolerance," where unlimited tolerance could enable the rise of intolerant ideologies. This paradox is particularly salient in debates surrounding extremist ideologies and counter-terrorism policies, as societies grapple with balancing free speech with public safety.

Free Speech in the Twenty-First Century: Key Controversies

While free speech remains a foundational principle, its practical application has become increasingly fraught. The following sections outline key controversies of the last decade that challenge traditional understandings of free expression. Over the next few chapters, we will be examining a few of these such as:

Chapter 5 will address Identity Politics and Pronouns: The rise of identity politics has highlighted tensions between free speech and inclusivity. Debates around the use of gender pronouns, for example, have sparked fierce controversies in academic and public spheres. Critics argue that enforcing pronoun use restricts free expression, while proponents contend that misgendering constitutes a form of harm; Butler, 1997). These debates underscore broader questions about whether free speech protections should extend to expressions perceived as discriminatory or harmful.

Chapter 6 will explore Academic Freedom: Universities have traditionally been bastions of free speech, fostering open debate and intellectual diversity. However, the past decade has seen growing concerns about "cancel culture" and the limits of academic freedom. Scholars have faced backlash for controversial views, leading to debates about whether such responses constitute accountability or censorship (Kempner et al., 2020). This tension reflects broader societal divides over the role of free speech in promoting versus challenging dominant ideologies.

Chapter 7 will explore Religion and Secularism: Religious expression occupies a unique position within free speech debates, often clashing with secular values. Controversies such as the Charlie Hebdo attacks in 2015 highlighted the risks of satirical depictions of religious figures, raising questions about the balance between free expression and respect for religious beliefs (Roy, 2017). Similarly, anti-blasphemy laws in certain countries continue to provoke international debate over the universality of free speech principles.

Chapter 8 will critically examine Counterterrorism and Extremism: Post-9/11 counter-terrorism legislation has increasingly intersected with free speech, as governments seek to curb extremist rhetoric online and offline. The UK's Prevent strategy, for example, has been criticised for its chilling effect on speech, particularly within Muslim communities (Qurashi, 2018). These policies reveal the challenges of reconciling free speech with national security in an era of globalised communication.

Navigating the Boundaries of Free Speech

The controversies outlined above illustrate the complexity of defining and defending free speech in contemporary society. While its foundational theories emphasise the value of open expression, practical realities often demand trade-offs between competing rights and interests.

The Harm Principle: Mill's harm principle, which permits restrictions on speech that causes direct harm to others, remains a central framework for navigating these dilemmas. However, defining "harm" in cases of psychological distress, discrimination, or radicalisation is often contentious (Waldron, 2012).

Technological Challenges: The rise of social media has transformed the dynamics of free speech, amplifying both its benefits and its risks. Platforms like Twitter and Facebook face ongoing scrutiny for their moderation practices, as they balance protecting speech with combating hate speech, disinformation, and harassment (Gillespie, 2018).

Global Perspectives: Free speech norms vary significantly across cultural and political contexts, complicating efforts to establish universal standards. For instance, while the United States maintains robust protections under the First Amendment, European countries often adopt a more restrictive approach, particularly concerning hate speech and Holocaust denial (Heinze, 2016).

Conclusion

Free speech remains one of the most critical yet contested principles of democratic societies. As explored throughout this chapter, its foundations lie in philosophical justifications rooted in the Enlightenment, such as John Stuart Mill's defence of the marketplace of ideas and Alexander Meiklejohn's emphasis on its necessity for democratic governance. These theories underscore the value of free expression as a mechanism for pursuing truth, protecting dissent, and fostering robust public discourse. However, the last decade has revealed that the practical application of these ideals is far from straightforward. Contemporary controversies expose the complexities of balancing free speech with competing societal values and demonstrate the challenges posed by evolving cultural, social, and technological landscapes.

The key controversies examined—identity politics and pronouns, academic freedom, religious expression, and counter-terrorism—highlight the fragility and nuance of free speech debates in the twenty-first century. The rise of identity politics, for example, brings into sharp focus the tension between free expression and inclusivity. Debates over gender pronouns and misgendering show how speech can affirm or harm individual identities, challenging the assumption that free expression is inherently neutral or universally beneficial. Similarly, controversies over academic freedom and so-called cancel culture have raised important questions about the limits of open inquiry. These debates reveal a tension between the need to protect diverse perspectives and the responsibility to create environments free from harm and discrimination.

Religious expression presents another complex intersection. Cases like the *Charlie Hebdo* attacks demonstrate the volatile clash between free speech and deeply held religious beliefs, raising important questions about the limits of satire and the balance between individual rights and communal respect. Likewise, the impact of counter-terrorism legislation, such as the UK's Prevent strategy, illustrates how national security imperatives can restrict freedom of expression, particularly in already marginalised communities. These examples demonstrate that free speech is not a static or universally agreed-upon concept but one that is constantly reshaped by political, cultural, and social dynamics.

Technological advances, particularly the rise of social media, have further complicated the boundaries of free speech. While platforms like Twitter and Facebook democratise access to expression, they also facilitate the spread of hate speech, misinformation, and harassment. These developments have sparked debates about the responsibilities of private corporations to moderate content and the potential for such moderation to become a form of censorship. In navigating these challenges, societies must grapple with the paradox of tolerance, as outlined by Karl Popper, and consider how best to address speech that threatens democratic norms or individual safety.

The need to navigate these tensions often returns to foundational principles such as Mill's harm principle, which suggests that speech should only be limited when it causes direct harm. However, defining harm—whether psychological, social, or political—remains a contentious issue. Global variations in free speech norms further complicate the discourse, as different societies prioritise values such as inclusivity, security, or autonomy in varying degrees. For instance, while the United States places a high premium on protecting almost all forms of speech under the First Amendment, European nations often take a more restrictive approach, particularly in relation to hate speech and Holocaust denial.

In addressing these controversies, this chapter underscores the importance of viewing free speech as a dynamic and context-dependent principle. While its theoretical foundations provide valuable guidance, the realities of the twenty-first century demand nuanced and flexible approaches to safeguarding this right. Subsequent chapters will delve deeper into the key intersections of free speech with identity politics, academic freedom, religion, and counter-terrorism, examining how these issues play out in practice and what they reveal about the evolving nature of free expression in modern society.

Ultimately, the debates surrounding free speech are emblematic of broader societal tensions over identity, power, and values. As these tensions continue to evolve, so too will the ways in which societies understand and navigate the boundaries of free expression. By engaging critically with these issues, we can better appreciate the complexities of this fundamental right and its role in shaping democratic and pluralistic societies.

Questions to Reflect On

1. Do classical theories of free speech—like Mill's marketplace of ideas—still hold up in the digital age of misinformation and online hate?
   - Reflect on whether unregulated expression still leads to truth and democratic engagement.
2. Should freedom of speech ever be limited to protect others from harm—and who should decide what constitutes "harm"?
   - Consider how the harm principle applies to issues like misgendering or extremist rhetoric.
3. How can societies balance free speech with competing values like inclusivity, national security, and respect for religious or cultural identities?
   - Think about tensions between expression and protection in diverse, pluralistic societies.

Bibliography

Barendt, E. 2005. *Freedom of Speech*. Oxford University Press.
Berlin, I. 1969. *Four Essays on Liberty*. Oxford University Press.
Butler, J. 1997. *Excitable Speech: A Politics of the Performative*. Routledge.
Fiss, O. 2009. *The Irony of Free Speech*. Harvard University Press.

Gillespie, T. 2018. *Custodians of the Internet: Platforms, Content Moderation, and the Hidden Decisions That Shape Social Media*. Yale University Press.

Heinze, E. 2016. *Hate Speech and Democratic Citizenship*. Oxford University Press.

Kempner, J., J. F. Merz, and C. L. Bosk. 2020. Forbidden Knowledge: Public Controversies and the Restriction of Scientific Research. *Science, Technology, & Human Values* 45 (2): 232–251.

Meiklejohn, A. 1948. *Free Speech and Its Relation to Self-Government*. Harper.

Mill, J. S. 1859. *On Liberty*. London: Penguin.

Popper, K. 1945. *The Open Society and Its Enemies*. Routledge.

Qurashi, F. 2018. The Prevent Strategy and the UK's War on Terror: Embedding Infrastructures of Surveillance in Muslim Communities. *Palgrave Communications* 4(1).

Roy, O. 2017. *Jihad and Death: The Global Appeal of Islamic State*. Hurst.

Sunstein, C. 2018. *#Republic: Divided Democracy in the Age of Social Media*. Princeton University Press.

Waldron, J. 2012. *The Harm in Hate Speech*. Harvard University Press.

Wilson, R. A., and M. K. Land. 2020. Hate Speech on Social Media: Content Moderation in Context. *Connecticut Law Review* 52: 1029.

CHAPTER 5

Politics and Pronouns and Free Speech

Abstract This chapter explores the role of gender pronouns within contemporary identity politics, situating their use at the intersection of language, personal identity, and socio-political activism. It traces the historical significance of pronouns in feminist and anti-subordination movements, while examining their modern function as tools of affirmation and resistance for transgender and non-binary individuals. The chapter analyses the psychological and social benefits of inclusive pronoun usage, as well as the challenges it presents—ranging from free speech debates and cultural resistance to the politicisation of language. Particular attention is paid to tensions between inclusivity and women's rights, highlighting feminist debates over shared spaces and linguistic shifts. Drawing on sociolinguistic research, case studies, and critical feminist perspectives, the chapter underscores the dual role of pronouns as both empowering and contested. Ultimately, it argues for a balanced approach that affirms diverse gender identities while respecting the need for safety, clarity, and thoughtful engagement across ideological divides.

Keywords **Marketplace of Ideas**—Mill's theory that open debate leads to the best ideas prevailing · **Autonomy**—The ability to govern oneself; linked to the right to express one's identity · **Democratic Function**—Free speech enables informed participation in political life · **Paradox of Tolerance**—Popper's idea that tolerating the intolerant can destroy tolerance · **Identity Politics**—Political positions based on social

E.-J. Peatfield, *Free Speech in Contention*,
https://doi.org/10.1007/978-3-031-94109-2_5

identities (e.g., gender, race, sexuality) · **Academic Freedom**—The liberty to teach and research without censorship or institutional pressure · **Blasphemy and Religion**—Speech that criticises religion; a contentious area in free speech debates · **Counterterrorism Laws**—Legal limits on speech in the name of preventing radicalisation

The Complexities of Gender Pronouns in Identity Politics

Gender pronouns have become a critical component in contemporary discussions surrounding identity politics, reflecting both the positive strides and significant challenges in addressing gender diversity. At their core, pronouns serve as linguistic tools, but their implications extend far beyond grammar into realms of personal identity, societal norms, and political activism. They act as markers of identity, acknowledgement, and respect, particularly for individuals who identify outside traditional gender binaries. The discourse surrounding pronouns not only highlights shifts, in societal attitudes towards gender, but also serves as a microcosm of broader debates about equality, representation, and the power of language. This essay explores the complexities of gender pronouns, analysing their roles, benefits, and controversies in identity politics through the lens of scholarly research and sociolinguistic studies.

Historical Context: Gender Pronouns and Social Movements

The historical evolution of gender pronouns highlights their embeddedness in broader socio-political movements. Hodson (2007) examines how pronouns were instrumental in the feminist movements of the 1790s, particularly in literary and rhetorical contexts. Women writers of the era strategically utilised personal pronouns to challenge patriarchal norms, advocating for the inclusion and recognition of women in public discourse. This historical precedent illustrates how pronouns have long been leveraged as tools for challenging systemic inequalities.

Similarly, Zietlow (2000) discusses how pronouns intersect with anti-subordination theories, suggesting that linguistic practices can either reinforce or dismantle power hierarchies. By examining historical patterns, we see that pronouns have consistently been more than grammatical constructs; they have functioned as instruments for asserting or contesting identities within a socio-political framework.

The Positive Impacts of Inclusive Pronoun Usage

One of the most significant advancements in the discourse surrounding gender pronouns is their role in fostering inclusivity. Mendes (2021) emphasises that the adoption of gender-neutral pronouns such as "they/them" represents a crucial step towards recognising and validating non-binary and transgender identities. These pronouns challenge the binary view of gender, promoting a more nuanced understanding of individual identity.

McGlashan and Fitzpatrick (2018) explore the experiences of transgender youth in navigating pronoun usage, highlighting the profound psychological benefits of inclusive language. For many transgender individuals, being addressed by their correct pronouns affirms their identity and fosters a sense of belonging. This recognition can mitigate feelings of dysphoria and social alienation, thereby contributing to mental well-being and social cohesion.

Furthermore, inclusive pronoun practices have broader implications for societal acceptance. Darr and Kibbey (2016) argue that linguistic neutrality, facilitated by gender-neutral pronouns, helps to deconstruct traditional gender norms. This deconstruction not only benefits individuals who identify outside the binary but also encourages society to question rigid gender roles, fostering greater equity and understanding.

Challenges and Controversies Surrounding Pronoun Usage

Despite the positive strides, the use of gender pronouns remains a contentious issue, often entangled in debates over free speech, cultural resistance, and practical implementation. One of the primary challenges is the perceived imposition of pronoun preferences in social and institutional settings. Critics argue that mandatory pronoun usage infringes on individual freedoms, particularly in contexts where linguistic changes are enforced through policies or legislation.

The resistance to pronoun inclusivity is often rooted in cultural and generational divides. Siewierska (2013) highlights how deeply ingrained gender distinctions are in linguistic structures across the world. These distinctions reflect broader societal norms, making the shift towards gender-neutral language a complex and, at times, polarised endeavour. The tension between tradition and progress is evident in the backlash against inclusive pronoun practices, which some perceive as an erosion of linguistic heritage.

Moreover, the reliance on pronouns to signify identity introduces ambiguities and potential conflicts. McGlashan and Fitzpatrick (2018) note that for some transgender individuals, the use of any pronoun can feel constraining, as it often fails to capture the fluidity and complexity of their identities. This highlights the limitations of language in fully accommodating diverse gender experiences, underscoring the need for broader cultural and structural changes beyond linguistic adjustments.

The Role of Pronouns in Marginalised Communities

Pronouns play a particularly significant role in the lives of marginalised groups, who often use language as a means of resisting systemic oppression. For transgender and non-binary individuals, pronoun preferences are not merely a matter of personal identity but also a form of political assertion. Mendes (2021) argues that the visibility of gender-neutral pronouns in public discourse signals a shift towards greater inclusivity and acknowledgement of marginalised voices.

Pronouns serve as a form of self-expression and validation, enabling individuals to assert their identities in a society that frequently marginalises non-conforming narratives. This assertion is crucial in combating erasure and creating spaces where diverse experiences are recognised and respected. However, this visibility often comes with risks, exposing individuals to heightened scrutiny and backlash. The politicisation of pronoun usage has, in many cases, led to targeted harassment and discrimination, particularly in environments where traditional gender norms are deeply entrenched. For example, misgendering or refusal to respect pronoun preferences can be a deliberate act of invalidation, reinforcing societal hierarchies that marginalise non-conforming individuals.

This underscores the dual-edged nature of pronouns as tools for both empowerment and vulnerability. While they provide a powerful means of asserting identity and challenging systemic inequities, they also expose individuals to potential harm, highlighting the ongoing struggle for acceptance and equality.

The Intersection of Feminism and Transgender Rights: A Pronoun Perspective

The intersection of feminism and transgender rights presents an additional layer of complexity in the discourse on pronouns. Price (2019) examines the tensions that sometimes arise between feminist movements and transgender advocacy, particularly in the context of shared spaces and language use. While many feminists embrace the use of gender-neutral pronouns as a means of fostering inclusivity and challenging restrictive gender norms, some argue that these practices can undermine women-only spaces by de-emphasising the unique experiences and struggles of cisgender women. This debate often highlights underlying disagreements about how gender is conceptualised and how best to address systemic inequities.

Price's analysis reveals that the debate over pronouns within feminist circles is far from uniform. Feminist movements encompass a range of perspectives, from radical feminists who prioritise sex-based rights to intersectional feminists who advocate for a more expansive understanding of gender inclusivity. These differing views often create tensions, as they require balancing the recognition of diverse gender identities with the protection of spaces historically reserved for women to address gendered oppression.

By framing pronoun usage as a site of negotiation rather than conflict, Price emphasises the potential for collaboration. Acknowledging both the importance of inclusivity and the need to protect vulnerable groups, such as women and transgender individuals, allows for a more nuanced approach. However, while inclusivity is vital, it is equally important to maintain women-only spaces where security and solidarity can be prioritised. These spaces often serve as critical environments for addressing the systemic inequalities and unique safety concerns faced by women, particularly in contexts where they remain disproportionately vulnerable to violence and discrimination. Striking a balance between inclusivity and the protection of such spaces requires thoughtful dialogue and a commitment to ensuring that no group's rights come at the expense of another's safety or dignity.

The Broader Implications for Identity Politics

The discourse surrounding gender pronouns is emblematic of larger trends in identity politics, particularly the tension between individual rights and collective norms. The increasing visibility of diverse gender identities has sparked broader discussions about the role of language in shaping societal values. As Darr and Kibbey (2016) note, pronoun debates often serve as proxies for larger ideological conflicts, reflecting the ongoing struggle between progressive and conservative worldviews. These conflicts are not merely about language but represent deeper cultural divides about the nature of identity, equality, and the role of institutions in reflecting societal change.

One of the most significant challenges in this context is the balance between inclusivity and practicality. While the adoption of gender-neutral pronouns is a positive step towards recognising diverse identities, it also requires significant cultural and institutional adjustments. These adjustments include revising educational curricula to promote understanding of non-binary identities, updating legal documents and administrative systems to accommodate pronoun preferences, and fostering greater awareness through public campaigns. Each of these changes demands resources, time, and a willingness to engage in often contentious dialogue.

However, amidst these efforts to embrace inclusivity, it is also essential to recognise and safeguard the rights and spaces of biological women. The inclusion of transgender women in certain contexts, such as women-only spaces and competitive sports, has raised significant concerns about fairness, safety, and the protection of opportunities for cisgender women. For example, sports organisations and governing bodies are grappling with how to maintain fair competition while respecting gender diversity. Similarly, women's shelters and other secure spaces must carefully balance inclusivity with the need to protect vulnerable women, many of whom seek refuge from gender-based violence.

Proponents of inclusivity must work collaboratively with advocates for women's rights to ensure that neither group is marginalised or disadvantaged. This requires thoughtful policies that account for biological realities while fostering respect for gender diversity. The ongoing negotiation of these issues underscores the evolving nature of identity politics, highlighting the need for a nuanced approach that balances inclusivity with the protection of women's spaces and opportunities. By addressing these tensions with sensitivity and care, society can work towards a future that respects and values all identities without compromising safety or fairness.

The Evolving Discourse on Gender Pronouns and Linguistic Innovation

The evolving discourse on gender pronouns also highlights the potential for linguistic innovation as a means of addressing societal changes. As Siewierska (2013) notes, language is inherently dynamic, adapting to reflect shifts in cultural and social norms. The emergence of new pronouns, such as "ze/hir" or neopronouns, demonstrates the capacity of language to accommodate diverse identities and challenge traditional norms. These innovations allow individuals to articulate their gender identity in ways that were previously unavailable, contributing to a broader cultural shift towards greater inclusivity.

However, the proliferation of pronoun options also raises questions about standardisation and accessibility. While linguistic innovation can promote inclusivity, it can also create confusion and resistance, particularly in contexts where new pronouns are not widely understood or accepted. For some, the rapid evolution of pronoun usage may feel overwhelming, especially when institutions and individuals are expected to adapt quickly. This highlights the need for ongoing dialogue, education, and sensitivity to ensure that linguistic changes are both meaningful and practical.

Importantly, the discourse on gender and pronouns must also respect the rights of women to make decisions about their spaces. Women have the right to choose whether or not to accept transgender women into their spaces, including shelters, support groups, and other environments specifically designed for biological women. This choice is not an act of exclusion but a reflection of the need to prioritise safety, shared experiences, and comfort within these spaces. For many women, particularly those who have faced gender-based violence, the ability to access female-only spaces without compromise is a critical issue of dignity and security.

While linguistic innovation and inclusivity are important, they must be pursued alongside a commitment to respecting the rights of all groups, including the rights of women to maintain autonomy over their spaces. These conversations must allow for diverse perspectives and the acknowledgement that inclusivity cannot come at the expense of individual rights and needs. Balancing these complex dynamics requires a thoughtful approach that recognises the nuances of identity, safety, and fairness.

Conclusion

The complexities surrounding gender pronouns underscore the broader cultural and societal shifts occurring in contemporary identity politics. On the one hand, the embrace of inclusive pronoun practices represents a significant milestone in the recognition and validation of diverse gender identities. On the other hand, the controversies and challenges associated with pronoun usage reveal deep-seated tensions within societal structures, linguistic norms, and political ideologies.

Inclusive pronoun usage has played a pivotal role in advancing discussions on gender equity and representation. Mendes (2021) and McGlashan and Fitzpatrick (2018) highlight the transformative potential of pronouns in fostering acceptance, reducing marginalisation, and affirming individual identities. For many, being recognised by their chosen pronouns is not just a matter of respect but a fundamental affirmation of their humanity. This affirmation has broader societal implications, challenging rigid gender binaries and encouraging more equitable social frameworks.

However, the road to widespread acceptance of inclusive pronouns is fraught with obstacles. Cultural resistance, as explored by Siewierska (2013), underscores how deeply ingrained gendered language can be, posing challenges to rapid change. Furthermore, the politicisation of pronouns has amplified ideological divides, with critics framing the push for inclusivity as an infringement on free speech or a departure from linguistic traditions. Such resistance highlights the need for carefully navigating the balance between advocating for inclusivity and addressing concerns about practical implementation and societal readiness.

The role of pronouns in identity politics extends beyond individual expression to address broader questions of power dynamics and social equity. For marginalised groups, pronouns are not just linguistic tools but powerful symbols of resistance against systemic oppression. As Mendes (2021), Price (2019), and Zietlow (2000) suggest, the visibility and recognition of diverse pronouns serve as a testament to the resilience and agency of these communities. Yet, this visibility also makes individuals more vulnerable to backlash, discrimination, and scrutiny, revealing the dual-edged nature of linguistic visibility.

In exploring the historical and contemporary dimensions of gender pronouns, this chapter has shed light on the complexities of their usage. From their roots in feminist and anti-subordination movements to their role in contemporary debates on inclusion and identity, pronouns encapsulate the evolving nature of societal values. They represent both progress and resistance, highlighting the intricate interplay between language, culture, and politics.

Looking forward, the discourse on gender pronouns will undoubtedly continue to evolve, reflecting ongoing shifts in societal norms and values. The challenges of standardising pronoun usage and addressing cultural resistance require sustained dialogue, education, and institutional support. At the same time, the potential for linguistic innovation offers opportunities to create a more inclusive and equitable society. By embracing the complexities of pronouns, we can foster a more nuanced understanding of identity and cultivate a society that values diversity, respect, and empathy.

In conclusion, the conversation surrounding gender pronouns is far from settled, but it remains central to the broader struggle for equity and inclusion. This ongoing dialogue reflects society's evolving understanding of identity and the role of language in shaping cultural values. By navigating these complexities with care and openness, we can ensure that language serves as a bridge rather than a barrier, fostering a society where all individuals feel seen, heard, and respected. The broader cultural shifts necessitated by these discussions present an opportunity to redefine inclusivity, ensuring that respect and dignity remain at the forefront of societal progress.

Questions to Reflect On

1. How can society balance the need for inclusive language with concerns about free speech, cultural tradition, or practical implementation?
   - Consider where rights to identity and expression might come into tension.
2. Do gender pronouns function more as personal identifiers, political tools, or both—and why does this distinction matter?
   - Reflect on how language shapes social power and recognition.

3. Can the push for pronoun inclusivity coexist with the protection of women-only spaces and rights—or are these goals inherently in conflict?
   - Explore how feminist and transgender rights might align or diverge.

Bibliography

Darr, B., and T. Kibbey. 2016. Pronouns and Thoughts on Neutrality: Gender Concerns in Modern Grammar. *Pursuit-the Journal of Undergraduate Research at the University of Tennessee* 7 (1): 10.

Hodson, J. 2007. Women Write the Rights of Woman: The Sexual Politics of the Personal Pronoun in the 1790s. *Language and Literature* 16 (3): 281–304.

McGlashan, H., and K. Fitzpatrick. 2018. I Use Any Pronouns, And I'm Questioning Everything Else: Transgender Youth and the Issue of Gender Pronouns. *Sex Education* 18 (3): 239–252.

Mendes, O. 2021. Gender-Neutral Pronouns: They Are Here to Stay. *Seton Hall Law Review* 52: 317.

Price, C. 2019. Women's Spaces, Women's Rights: Feminism and the Transgender Rights Movement. *Marquette Law Review* 103: 1509.

Siewierska, A. 2013. Gender Distinctions in Independent Personal Pronouns. *The World Atlas of Language Structures Online*.

Zietlow, R. E. 2000. Beyond the Pronoun: Toward an Anti-Subordinating Method of Process. *Texas Journal of Women & Law* 10: 1.

CHAPTER 6

Academic Free Speech

Abstract This chapter critically examines academic free speech in the UK, exploring its legal, historical, and cultural dimensions in an era marked by increasing social and political polarisation. Drawing on key literature and recent legislation—including the Higher Education (Freedom of Speech) Act 2023—it analyses the tensions between free intellectual inquiry and the drive for inclusivity, institutional accountability, and student protection. The chapter traces the evolution of academic freedom from post-war liberal values to its contemporary entanglement with cancel culture, decolonisation debates, and no-platforming controversies. It also considers the role of universities as both protectors of scholarly independence and stewards of inclusive, respectful environments. By engaging with diverse perspectives on academic responsibility, student expression, and the risks of institutional overreach, the chapter offers a nuanced framework for navigating the competing imperatives of free speech and equity in higher education. It concludes with recommendations for fostering academic cultures that support open inquiry while respecting the rights and dignity of all participants.

Keywords **Pronouns**—Words used to refer to people (e.g., he, she, they), significant in expressing gender identity · **Non-Binary**—A gender identity outside the male/female binary · **Inclusivity**—Practices that recognise and respect diverse identities · **Misgendering**—Referring to someone using incorrect pronouns; often seen as a form of disrespect ·

E.-J. Peatfield, *Free Speech in Contention*,
https://doi.org/10.1007/978-3-031-94109-2_6

Linguistic Norms—Established rules and habits of language use, including gender · **Trans Rights**—Legal and social rights advocating for transgender individuals · **Speech vs. Harm Debate**—Tension between free expression and its potential to cause emotional harm · **Feminist Perspectives**—Views that sometimes diverge on how gender inclusivity affects women's rights

Introduction

Academic free speech is a cornerstone of higher education, shaping the boundaries of knowledge creation, dissemination, and critique. In the UK, this principle has come under increasing scrutiny, with debates on its limitations, responsibilities, and intersections with broader societal values. The evolving political, social, and cultural climate has heightened these debates, as concerns about inclusivity, cancel culture, and ideological bias intersect with the foundational ideal of open intellectual inquiry. This chapter explores the complexities of academic free speech within the UK context, critically engaging with existing literature to provide a foundation for further inquiry.

Key contributions by scholars such as Bérubé and Ruth (2022), Cram and Fenwick (2018), and Simpson (2020) serve as the basis for this analysis, supplemented by insights into contemporary challenges and historical precedents. For example, the work of Cram and Fenwick (2018) highlights the delicate balance between protecting academic freedoms and fostering an inclusive environment, pointing to cases where perceived tensions have led to public and institutional backlash. Similarly, Simpson's (2020) discussion of academic self-censorship raises questions about how institutional pressures and societal expectations shape the scope of permissible discourse.

This chapter also examines how historical precedents, such as the student protests of the 1960s and the rise of critical theory in UK universities, provide context for the current landscape. While these movements championed academic freedom as a vehicle for progress, they also underscored the persistent tension between the academy's commitment to free expression and its responsibility to broader societal values, such as equality and respect.

Through a critical review of this evolving discourse, the chapter considers how the UK legal framework—particularly the Higher Education (Freedom of Speech) Act 2023—impacts academic freedom, addressing both its opportunities and challenges. The chapter aims to provide a nuanced understanding of this contentious issue, offering a platform for further academic and policy-oriented exploration.

Defining Academic Free Speech

Academic free speech, while closely related to free speech more broadly, possesses distinct characteristics rooted in the university's mission to pursue truth. It operates within a unique context where the pursuit of knowledge, critical thinking, and intellectual development are prioritised. Simpson (2020) articulates the nuanced relationship between academic freedom and free speech, emphasising the former's role in fostering an environment conducive to rigorous inquiry and debate. He argues that academic freedom requires a framework that balances individual expression with institutional goals, ensuring that freedom is exercised responsibly. This balance is particularly significant in navigating contentious issues, where the potential for conflict must be managed in a way that preserves open discourse while avoiding harm to the academic community.

Bérubé and Ruth (2022) further elaborate on this point, noting that academic free speech is not an absolute right but rather a privilege bound by ethical and professional standards. They stress that within the academic sphere, speech must be guided by principles of integrity, evidence-based argumentation, and respect for others' intellectual contributions. Their work underscores the importance of maintaining a democratic and inclusive academic culture, particularly in contexts where race, gender, and identity intersect with speech rights. For example, they highlight how unchecked free speech can sometimes marginalise underrepresented voices, undermining the inclusive ethos that universities aim to foster.

These perspectives highlight the dual nature of academic free speech as both an individual right and a collective responsibility. The individual scholar's right to freely express ideas must coexist with the university's obligation to promote respectful and meaningful dialogue. This interplay raises critical questions about the boundaries of permissible speech and the mechanisms through which universities can safeguard both intellectual freedom and inclusivity. Ultimately, the complexities of academic free speech challenge institutions to constantly reassess their policies and practices, ensuring they remain aligned with their foundational mission of advancing knowledge and promoting equity.

Historical Context and Legal Frameworks

We spoke about the limitations of free speech and what constitutes free speech in Chapter 1. However, the UK's approach to academic free speech is deeply influenced by its legal and cultural history, which continues to shape debates in contemporary higher education. Cram and Fenwick (2018) provide a comprehensive analysis of the legislative framework protecting free speech and academic freedom in universities. They highlight the significance of the *Education (No. 2) Act 1986*, which imposes a duty on higher education institutions to uphold free speech within the law, alongside more recent legislation such as the *Higher Education (Freedom of Speech) Act 2023*. These laws form the backbone of legal protections for academic expression, but their interpretation and implementation have raised complex questions about the balance between freedom and responsibility.

The challenges associated with implementing these protections have become increasingly visible in recent years. The rise of no-platforming and cancel culture has sparked heated debates about the boundaries of acceptable speech on campus. Oleksiyenko and Jackson (2021) argue that these phenomena are not merely confined to academia but reflect broader societal tensions, including the erosion of trust in expertise and the proliferation of misinformation in the ***post-truth era***. Their analysis suggests that academic free speech is under strain, caught between demands for greater inclusivity and the risks posed by disinformation and divisive rhetoric.

We must also consider the role of institutional policies in navigating these tensions. Universities face the challenging task of balancing their legal obligation to protect free speech with their responsibility to foster safe and inclusive learning environments. This includes addressing the complexities of speech that, while legally permissible, may perpetuate harm or marginalisation. Oleksiyenko and Jackson (2021) advocate for a re-evaluation of academic free speech frameworks, emphasising the need for universities to adopt a nuanced approach that acknowledges the shifting dynamics of social and cultural discourse.

The *Higher Education (Freedom of Speech) Act 2023* represents a significant legislative development in the UK, aimed at strengthening protections for free speech within higher education institutions. The Act builds on existing legislation, such as the *Education (No. 2) Act 1986*, by imposing new duties on universities and students' unions to uphold and promote free speech. One of its key provisions is the creation of a Director for Freedom of Speech and Academic Freedom within the Office for Students (OfS), tasked with monitoring compliance and addressing breaches of these responsibilities.

The Act explicitly reinforces the importance of free speech as essential to academic inquiry, critical thinking, and intellectual diversity. It includes measures to ensure that individuals, including staff, students, and visiting speakers, are not unlawfully denied a platform based on their views, provided they adhere to the law. The legislation also grants individuals the right to seek legal redress if they believe their free speech rights have been violated, introducing potential financial and reputational consequences for institutions that fail to comply.

Critics, however, argue that the Act risks fostering a culture of litigation and may unintentionally limit speech by increasing bureaucratic oversight. Nonetheless, it underscores the UK government's commitment to safeguarding free expression in academia amidst evolving societal and cultural debates.

Contemporary Challenges

One of the most pressing challenges to academic free speech in the UK is the tension between inclusivity and the protection of controversial viewpoints. This issue has gained prominence as universities seek to balance their commitment to diversity and inclusion with their role as spaces for open intellectual debate. Honeycutt, Stevens, and Kaufmann (2023) explore this dynamic through a survey of faculty attitudes, revealing a significant divide in perceptions of free expression on campus. While many academics support the principle of free speech in theory, they also express concerns about its potential to perpetuate harm against marginalised groups, particularly in a context where power dynamics and historical inequalities remain entrenched.

This tension is particularly pronounced in debates over decolonising the curriculum. Advocates of decolonisation argue for the inclusion of diverse perspectives and the critical examination of historical injustices embedded within academic disciplines. However, these efforts often encounter pushback, with critics alleging that they amount to censorship or the erosion of traditional academic standards. Additionally, academics engaging with controversial or politically sensitive subjects may find themselves vulnerable to spurious claims of bias, misconduct, or unprofessionalism, particularly in the polarised landscape of public discourse. These claims can threaten careers, undermine intellectual inquiry, and discourage researchers from addressing contentious issues.

Bérubé and Ruth (2022) emphasise the importance of navigating these debates with care, ensuring that equity initiatives do not unintentionally suppress legitimate academic inquiry. They argue that universities must also actively protect academics and researchers from unwarranted accusations, which can arise from their work on controversial topics. Clear institutional policies and robust support mechanisms are necessary to safeguard against the misuse of complaints or legal threats intended to silence scholars.

Ultimately, the challenge lies in addressing the lived experiences of marginalised groups while maintaining the core mission of higher education as a place of exploration, critique, and discovery. This includes fostering environments where diverse perspectives can coexist, controversial ideas can be rigorously debated, and academics are shielded from attempts to stifle inquiry through spurious claims. Striking this balance is crucial for sustaining both inclusivity and academic freedom in the UK's evolving higher education landscape.

The Role of Universities

Universities play a pivotal role in upholding academic free speech, acting as both guarantors of individual rights and stewards of the public good. Turk (2014) explores the institutional dimensions of academic freedom, arguing that universities must resist external pressures that threaten their autonomy. These pressures include political interference, market-driven priorities, and public backlash against controversial research or teaching. Without such resistance, the core mission of higher education—to pursue truth and foster critical thinking—can become compromised.

Simpson (2020) echoes this sentiment, asserting that universities have a moral obligation to defend academic free speech even in the face of societal opposition. He contends that this requires a commitment to institutional values that prioritise intellectual diversity and rigorous debate over conformity and convenience. Upholding these values is essential not only for preserving academic freedom but also for equipping students and academics to navigate the complexities of an increasingly polarised world.

One of the most pressing challenges to academic free speech in the UK is the tension between inclusivity and the protection of controversial viewpoints. This issue has gained prominence as universities seek to balance their commitment to diversity and inclusion with their role as spaces for open intellectual debate. Honeycutt, Stevens, and Kaufmann (2023) examine this dynamic through a survey of faculty attitudes, revealing a significant divide in perceptions of free expression on campus. While many academics support the principle of free speech, they also express concerns about its potential to perpetuate harm against marginalised groups, particularly in a context where power dynamics and historical inequalities remain entrenched.

This tension extends to students, who play a critical role in shaping the campus free speech landscape. Universities must protect students' rights to express diverse viewpoints without fear of retaliation or harassment, even when their perspectives diverge from the majority or challenge prevailing norms. This includes protecting students from actions by peers that may seek to silence, intimidate, or exclude them based on their beliefs. Instances of online abuse, organised protests designed to shut down speakers, or peer-driven efforts to ostracise individuals for controversial opinions highlight the challenges of fostering a truly open and respectful academic environment.

At the same time, fostering free speech among students must be balanced with the need to create an inclusive environment where no student feels marginalised or unsafe. Universities must provide clear policies and education on free speech rights and responsibilities to help students understand the boundaries between robust debate and harmful speech. Bérubé and Ruth (2022) argue that free speech cannot thrive unless students feel confident that their own voices will be heard and that expressing unpopular or contentious ideas will not expose them to undue harm or exclusion.

To achieve this balance, universities should develop mechanisms such as facilitated dialogues, mediation programmes, and supportive grievance processes that address both free speech concerns and allegations of harm. These measures can help protect students from being silenced while ensuring that all voices—particularly those from marginalised backgrounds—are given the opportunity to contribute to academic discourse. Ultimately, protecting students from undue peer pressures and fostering a culture of mutual respect are essential for preserving free speech and promoting intellectual diversity in UK universities.

International Comparisons

While the UK faces unique challenges, it is also part of a broader global conversation about academic free speech. Oleksiyenko and Jackson (2021) compare the UK context with other countries, highlighting both similarities and differences in how academic freedom is conceptualised and practised. They observe that while the UK's legal framework offers strong protections for academic freedom, its effectiveness is often undermined by cultural and political dynamics, including rising intolerance of dissenting voices, and increased external pressures on universities. These challenges are not confined to the UK, as academic institutions globally navigate tensions between legal guarantees of free expression and the realities of political, social, and economic constraints.

Bérubé and Ruth (2022) expand on this analysis, emphasising the importance of understanding how national and global factors intersect to influence academic free speech. They argue that the global rise of authoritarianism and populism poses a profound threat to academic freedom by fostering environments of censorship, self-censorship, and fear of reprisal for controversial research or views. Moreover, they stress that this is a collective issue, requiring international collaboration and solidarity within the academic community. Without such coordinated responses, the erosion of academic freedom in one country risks setting a dangerous precedent for others, weakening global intellectual inquiry and open debate.

Moving Forward

Addressing the challenges to academic free speech in the UK requires a multifaceted approach that balances the protection of free expression with the need for inclusivity and respect. Honeycutt, Stevens, and Kaufmann (2023) propose several strategies to foster a campus culture that values free speech. These include promoting open dialogue between diverse perspectives, creating spaces where marginalised voices are empowered to contribute without fear of reprisal, and establishing clear, consistent guidelines for resolving conflicts related to speech. By implementing these strategies, institutions can ensure that academic freedom thrives while maintaining a respectful and supportive environment for all members of the academic community. These recommendations align closely with Cram and Fenwick's (2018) call for universities to adopt stronger institutional policies that explicitly balance free speech with inclusivity, ensuring that debates remain robust yet respectful.

In addition to institutional policies, broader advocacy and public engagement are critical in defending academic free speech. Turk (2014) argues that universities have a responsibility not only to protect these rights within their campuses but also to champion their importance in societal discourse. This involves challenging common misconceptions about academic freedom, particularly the idea that it fosters division, and instead highlighting its essential role in advancing knowledge, promoting critical inquiry, and supporting democratic ideals. Institutions must actively communicate the value of academic free speech as a public good, emphasising its contribution to societal progress and innovation. By taking an active role in public debates, universities can strengthen the case for academic freedom while fostering greater understanding of its critical role in democracy.

Conclusion

Academic free speech in the UK is at a critical juncture, shaped by a complex interplay of legal, cultural, and institutional factors. As this chapter has demonstrated, the principle of academic freedom is both a right and a responsibility, requiring careful navigation of competing values and priorities. By drawing on the insights of scholars such as Bérubé and Ruth (2022), Cram and Fenwick (2018), and Simpson (2020), this analysis provides a foundation for understanding and addressing the challenges facing academic free speech in the UK today.

In recent years, the concept of academic free speech has been increasingly contested in response to a range of societal pressures. These include the growing politicisation of university campuses, debates over the limits of free expression, and the role of universities in addressing issues of equity and inclusion. As highlighted by Cram and Fenwick (2018), the tension between promoting open dialogue and maintaining inclusive environments is particularly pronounced, with universities often struggling to strike a balance. The challenge is further compounded by legislative changes, such as the Higher Education (Freedom of Speech) Bill, which has sought to codify the obligations of universities in safeguarding free speech while raising concerns about potential overreach.

Cultural shifts also play a pivotal role in shaping academic free speech. Simpson (2020) argues that the rise of "cancel culture" and online activism has created new dynamics for academic debate, where individuals may feel silenced by fear of public backlash or institutional reprimand. While these movements aim to challenge harmful or exclusionary practices, they also risk curbing legitimate academic inquiry and stifling dissent.

To address these challenges, universities, policymakers, and academics must work collaboratively to uphold academic freedom. This requires developing institutional policies that are transparent and consistent, fostering cultures of respectful debate, and ensuring robust support for those who face pressures to conform. Only through such collective efforts can higher education remain a space for rigorous inquiry, critical debate, and social progress.

Questions for Reflection

1. How should universities balance the protection of academic free speech with their duty to foster inclusive and respectful learning environments?

    – Consider how both aims might come into conflict in practice.

2. Does the Higher Education (Freedom of Speech) Act 2023 strengthen or undermine academic freedom in UK universities? Why?

    – Reflect on the potential benefits and risks of legislating speech on campus.

3. Can controversial or offensive academic viewpoints be part of legitimate scholarly debate, or should there be limits—and who decides where those limits lie?

    – Explore who holds power in determining academic boundaries.

Bibliography

Bérubé, M., and J. Ruth. 2022. *It's Not Free Speech: Race, Democracy, and the Future of Academic Freedom*. JHU Press.

Cram, I., and H. Fenwick. 2018. Protecting Free Speech and Academic Freedom in Universities.

Honeycutt, N., S. T. Stevens, and E. Kaufmann. 2023. The Academic Mind in 2022: What Faculty Think About Free Expression and Academic Freedom on Campus.

Oleksiyenko, A. V., and L. Jackson. 2021. Freedom of Speech, Freedom to Teach, Freedom to Learn: The Crisis of Higher Education in the Post-truth Era. *Educational Philosophy and Theory* 53 (11): 1057–1062.

Simpson, R. M. 2020. The Relation Between Academic Freedom and Free Speech. *Ethics* 130 (3): 287–319.

Turk, J. L., ed. 2014. *Academic Freedom in Conflict: The Struggle over Free Speech Rights in the University*. James Lorimer & Company.

CHAPTER 7

Religious Freedom and Free Speech

Abstract This chapter explores the complex and often fraught relationship between religious freedom and free speech in modern democratic societies. Drawing on legal, philosophical, and sociopolitical perspectives, it examines how these two fundamental rights—each essential to democratic life—can collide, particularly in multicultural contexts where diverse values and belief systems coexist. The chapter begins by outlining theoretical frameworks from scholars such as Mill, Magarian, and Parekh, highlighting both the democratic potential and risks of religious expression in public discourse. It then critically analyses legal tensions through the lens of international human rights law and global case studies, including the contentious application of blasphemy laws and the use of religious rhetoric in restricting reproductive rights. Through key examples such as the Howl obscenity trial, the chapter also explores how religiously motivated censorship intersects with debates on artistic freedom, misinformation, and the role of digital platforms. Furthermore, it considers the growing influence of populist movements that weaponise religion and free speech to exclude minority voices and polarise public debate. Ultimately, the chapter argues for nuanced, context-sensitive legal and cultural frameworks that uphold both freedoms while preventing their misuse. It emphasises the importance of dialogue, education, and international cooperation in managing these intersecting rights in an increasingly diverse and interconnected world.

E.-J. Peatfield, *Free Speech in Contention*,
https://doi.org/10.1007/978-3-031-94109-2_7

Keywords **Academic Freedom**—The right to research, publish, and teach without interference · **Higher Education (Freedom of Speech) Act 2023**—UK legislation aimed at reinforcing free speech in universities · **Safe Spaces**—Campus environments designed to protect students from harm or discrimination · **No-Platforming**—barring individuals from speaking at universities due to controversial views · **Self-Censorship**—Withholding opinions out of fear of backlash or professional consequences · **Ideological Bias**—When particular political or cultural views dominate academic environments · **Institutional Autonomy**—Universities' independence from political and commercial pressures · **Democratic Inquiry**—The pursuit of knowledge through open, critical, and diverse debate

Introduction

The intersection of religious freedom and free speech represents a nuanced and often contentious area of modern democratic societies, where competing rights frequently collide in ways that challenge social harmony and legal principles. At its core, this intersection reflects the struggle to balance two deeply held values: the right to express and practice one's faith freely and the right to articulate ideas, opinions, and criticisms—even when they may be deemed offensive or controversial. These tensions become especially pronounced in multicultural and pluralistic societies, where diverse worldviews and belief systems coexist, often within close proximity, and where the potential for conflict between freedoms is ever-present.

This chapter explores the delicate balance between the right to express religious beliefs and the protection of free speech. It considers how these freedoms are conceptualised and operationalised in theory and practice, drawing upon insights from political philosophy, sociology, and legal studies. By investigating the theoretical underpinnings of these rights, the chapter examines foundational principles such as John Stuart Mill's arguments on liberty, Rawlsian justice, and multicultural theories advanced by scholars like Bhikhu Parekh and Will Kymlicka. These perspectives illuminate how societies have sought to reconcile individual freedoms with broader collective interests.

The discussion also delves into legal precedents that have shaped the boundaries of religious freedom and free speech. Key cases, both domestic and international, illustrate the often complex and context-dependent judgements made by courts in navigating disputes that pit religious sensibilities against free expression. Notable examples include blasphemy laws, hate speech regulations, and the legal challenges surrounding religious attire and symbols in public spaces.

Finally, this chapter considers the societal implications of these freedoms, particularly in the light of growing religious diversity and the rise of populist movements that often exploit such tensions. It critically examines how the interplay between religious freedom and free speech shapes public discourse, social cohesion, and the broader commitment to democratic values.

Theoretical Frameworks: The Tension Between Freedoms

Religious freedom and free speech are both enshrined as fundamental human rights in international legal frameworks such as the Universal Declaration of Human Rights (UDHR). Article 18 of the UDHR guarantees the right to freedom of thought, conscience, and religion, while Article 19 affirms the right to freedom of opinion and expression. These principles collectively underscore the importance of allowing individuals to express their religious beliefs freely while ensuring that diverse viewpoints are respected within a democratic society. However, as Gey (2000, p. 379) observes, conflicts often arise when religious speech infringes on other rights or promotes harm, posing challenges to legal and moral boundaries. For instance, when religious expression includes hate speech or incitement to violence, societies must grapple with determining where the line between free speech and harmful conduct is drawn. Gey's analysis highlights the importance of distinguishing between protected religious expression and speech that undermines public order or democratic principles.

Magarian (2011, p. 119) builds on this by examining how religious arguments intersect with democratic free speech theory, offering a nuanced perspective on the role of religious rhetoric in public discourse. He posits that religious rhetoric can enhance democratic dynamism by introducing diverse perspectives and challenging dominant ideologies. For example, religious movements have historically played a crucial role in advocating for social justice, such as during the US civil rights movement, where leaders like Martin Luther King Jr. drew on religious principles to promote equality and human dignity. This demonstrates the positive potential of religious speech to inspire social change and enrich democratic debate.

However, Magarian also cautions against the risks associated with religious speech, particularly when it monopolises or suppresses alternative viewpoints. When religious rhetoric becomes overly dominant, it can crowd out secular or minority perspectives, potentially leading to a form of ideological hegemony that undermines democratic pluralism. This risk is especially pronounced in cases where religious groups wield significant political power, using their influence on shape legislation or public policy in ways that may not reflect the broader society's values. For instance, debates over reproductive rights, LGBTQ+ protections, and educational curricula often reveal tensions between religious advocacy and the rights of other groups.

These complexities highlight the need for balancing inclusivity with equitable representation in democratic spaces. While religious expression can contribute to a vibrant public sphere, it must not come at the expense of marginalising other voices or violating fundamental human rights. Legal frameworks, therefore, play a crucial role in maintaining this balance, ensuring that religious freedom and free speech coexist without undermining the principles of democracy and equality.

Blasphemy Laws and Global Implications

Blasphemy laws exemplify the tension between religious freedom and free speech, serving as a focal point for debates on how to balance these fundamental rights. Holzapfel (2014, p. 597) argues that international blasphemy laws often privilege religious sensitivities over free expression, stifling open debate and disproportionately affecting minority voices. In many countries, these laws are framed as a means of protecting religious harmony or preventing societal unrest. However, Holzapfel critiques such laws as a form of censorship that undermines democratic values, particularly in contexts where they are weaponised to silence dissent, suppress criticism of dominant religious groups, or target vulnerable populations. For instance, in countries like Pakistan, blasphemy laws have been used to disproportionately affect religious minorities, such as Christians and Hindus, who face accusations that often lack substantiated evidence but result in severe punishments, including imprisonment or even death sentences. Or Iran and Syria where Christians have been murdered and their places of worship targeted. Such applications of blasphemy laws reveal their potential to reinforce societal inequalities and inhibit open discourse.

Mondal (2016, pp. 3–24) provides a complementary perspective, analysing how freedom of expression and religious freedom coexist in multicultural societies. He explores the complex interplay between these rights, noting that both can be weaponised to further political or ideological agendas. On the one hand, freedom of expression can be used to incite hatred or promote offensive rhetoric targeting specific religious communities. Conversely, religious freedom can be invoked to justify discriminatory practices, such as denying equal rights to women or LGBTQ+ individuals under the guise of adhering to religious doctrine. One prominent example is the pro-life movement, which demonstrates how religious rhetoric is frequently employed to justify restrictions on women's rights, particularly their reproductive autonomy.

The pro-life movement, deeply rooted in religious ideologies, has used freedom of speech and religious freedom to argue against abortion and advocate for the criminalisation of what they consider the "murder" of unborn children. These groups have exerted noteworthy influence on public policy in countries like the United States, where religiously motivated lobbying efforts have led to the erosion of abortion rights in many states. For instance, the 2022 overturning of *Roe v. Wade* by the US Supreme Court marked a significant victory for pro-life advocates but simultaneously stripped millions of women of their constitutional right to access safe and legal abortions. By framing their position as a matter of moral and religious conviction, the pro-life movement often sidelines the voices of women, particularly those from marginalised communities, whose access to health care is disproportionately impacted by these restrictions.

Pro-life activists frequently leverage free speech protections to stage protests outside clinics, sometimes employing aggressive tactics to shame and intimidate women seeking abortions. These demonstrations highlight the tensions between the right to protest and the right to privacy, with many arguing that such actions cross the line into harassment. Furthermore, the movement often claims religious freedom to justify restrictive laws, such as mandatory waiting periods, ultrasounds, or counselling sessions designed to dissuade women from obtaining abortions. Critics argue that these measures not only undermine women's agency over their own bodies but also reflect an imposition of religious values onto secular legal frameworks, creating a climate of coercion rather than choice.

Mondal's call for a contextual approach is particularly relevant in addressing these issues. He advocates for legal frameworks that not only uphold the principles of free expression and religious freedom but also account for cultural diversity, power dynamics, and the potential for abuse. This includes recognising how religious freedom claims can be wielded to curtail the rights of others, as seen in the pro-life movement's efforts to restrict reproductive rights. Such frameworks must ensure that free speech is not used as a cover for hate speech, intimidation, or the erosion of individual freedoms, and that religious freedom does not serve as a pretext for oppression. In doing so, societies can better navigate the complexities of these intersecting rights, fostering both inclusion and democratic integrity.

Contemporary Cases; Howl on Trial

The battle for free expression has a storied history, as illustrated by Morgan (2021). Through the lens of landmark cases like *Howl on Trial*, Morgan examines how free speech has been defended against censorship attempts rooted in religious or moral objections. These cases underscore the enduring importance of safeguarding artistic and literary expression as a cornerstone of democratic societies. The trial of Allen Ginsberg's poem *Howl* in 1957, for example, highlighted the tension between creative freedom and societal norms. Prosecutors labelled the poem obscene due to its candid depictions of sexuality and critiques of consumerist culture, reflecting broader anxieties about post-war social change. However, the court ultimately ruled in favour of Ginsberg, establishing a precedent that protected artistic works even when they provoked moral or religious discomfort. Morgan argues that such cases are pivotal in affirming the principle that free expression includes the right to challenge dominant ideologies, particularly those upheld by religious or conservative institutions.

In contemporary times, the landscape of free speech has grown even more complex. Sunstein (2021) highlights the proliferation of misinformation and its implications for free speech, a challenge compounded by the rise of social media and digital platforms. He argues that falsehoods, particularly those rooted in religious or ideological zeal, pose significant challenges to democratic discourse. Misinformation campaigns have exploited the protections afforded to free speech, spreading conspiracy theories, pseudoscience, and hate speech under the guise of individual liberty. Sunstein draws attention to examples like the spread of anti-vaccine rhetoric or climate change denial, where religious or ideological groups disseminate false claims that have tangible consequences for public health and policy.

Sunstein's work underscores the necessity of robust mechanisms to counter deception while preserving the essential freedoms of speech and religion. He emphasises the role of media literacy and fact-checking initiatives in empowering individuals to critically evaluate information. Furthermore, he advocates for platform accountability, arguing that tech companies have a moral and social responsibility to curb the spread of harmful content without infringing on users' rights. The challenge lies in striking a balance between combating misinformation and avoiding censorship, particularly when such actions might disproportionately impact minority or dissenting voices.

The intersection of religious expression and misinformation further complicates these debates. For instance, in cases where religious groups promote false narratives, such as faith-healing claims that discourage medical intervention, society must navigate the fine line between respecting religious freedom and protecting public welfare. Sunstein emphasises that unchecked misinformation driven by religious fervour has the potential to erode social cohesion and democratic principles by creating distrust and fostering division. This dynamic illustrates the ongoing need for legal and cultural frameworks that defend free speech while addressing its potential for misuse in an increasingly interconnected and polarised world.

Populism, Religion, and Emotional Appeals

Yilmaz and Morieson (2021, p. 272) examine the interplay of populism, religion, and emotions in shaping public discourse. Their systematic literature review reveals how populist movements often exploit religious sentiments to galvanise support, framing themselves as defenders of traditional values against perceived threats. By appealing to religious identities and invoking emotional narratives, populist leaders frequently position themselves as protectors of cultural heritage, morality, and national identity. This tactic not only strengthens their political base but also polarises societies by creating an "us versus them" dynamic. In doing so, populism weaponises religious freedom and free speech, transforming them into tools for furthering exclusionary and divisive agendas.

One prominent example is the rhetoric employed by right-wing populist leaders in Europe and the United States. Leaders like Viktor Orbán in Hungary and Donald Trump in the United States have consistently invoked Christian identity to frame their policies and consolidate support among religious conservatives. Orbán, for instance, has portrayed himself as a defender of "Christian Europe" against the perceived threat of Muslim migration, using religion as a rallying point for anti-immigration policies. Similarly, Trump's speeches frequently appealed to evangelical Christians, presenting himself as a champion of religious freedom while simultaneously criticising policies that protect minority groups. Yilmaz and Morieson highlight that such narratives resonate deeply with specific segments of the population, tapping into fears of cultural erosion and moral decline.

These dynamics illustrate the complex ways in which religious freedom and free speech intersect with broader socio-political trends. Populist movements often invoke free speech as a defence against criticism, framing their controversial rhetoric as an exercise of their democratic rights. However, their reliance on religious sentiment often blurs the line between legitimate expression and exclusionary ideology. For instance, populist rhetoric frequently targets minority religious groups, using freedom of expression to justify discriminatory practices or hate speech. This raises critical questions about the limits of both freedoms in safeguarding democratic integrity. Should free speech protections extend to rhetoric that undermines the rights of others, and where should the boundary between religious freedom and societal harm be drawn?

Furthermore, Yilmaz and Morieson argue that the emotional appeal of populist discourse complicates efforts to challenge it through reasoned debate. By leveraging religious and emotional narratives, populist leaders create an environment where policy discussions are overshadowed by identity politics and cultural anxieties. This not only undermines rational discourse but also risks eroding public trust in democratic institutions. As such, the interplay of populism, religion, and emotions highlights the fragile balance between protecting fundamental freedoms and preventing their misuse in ways that threaten social cohesion and equality.

Ultimately, their work underscores the importance of critical engagement with the socio-political dimensions of free speech and religious freedom. Legal and cultural frameworks must not only uphold these rights but also address their potential for exploitation in populist movements. By doing so, societies can better navigate the challenges posed by the intersection of religion, politics, and emotions in contemporary public discourse.

Conclusion

The relationship between religious freedom and free speech is inherently complex, requiring careful navigation to uphold democratic values while respecting cultural and religious diversity. These two fundamental freedoms, enshrined in international human rights frameworks, often intersect in ways that reflect broader social, political, and cultural dynamics. As the works of Gey, Holzapfel, Magarian, Mondal, Morgan, Sunstein, and Yilmaz and Morieson illustrate, this interplay is multifaceted, involving tensions that extend beyond abstract legal principles into the lived realities of individuals and communities.

One key takeaway from these works is the importance of recognising that neither freedom exists in isolation. Religious freedom, while a cornerstone of democratic societies, must not be used to justify discrimination or suppress dissenting views. Similarly, free speech should not be an unchecked license for hate speech, misinformation, or the erosion of social cohesion. Gey and Holzapfel highlight how these tensions manifest in legal frameworks, particularly in contexts where religious sensitivities are used to justify censorship or where free speech protections are exploited to harm marginalised groups. These cases underscore the need for legal mechanisms that protect both freedoms while preventing their misuse.

The works of Magarian (2011) and Mondal (2016) further illustrate how these freedoms interact within democratic spaces, where inclusivity and representation must be carefully balanced. Religious rhetoric, while contributing valuable perspectives to public discourse, can become exclusionary or suppress alternative viewpoints when monopolised by dominant groups. This dynamic is evident in the strategies of the pro-life movement, which frequently invokes religious freedom to restrict women's reproductive rights, and in populist movements that weaponise religion and emotion to polarise societies. Yilmaz and Morieson's (2021) exploration of populism demonstrates how these tactics can undermine democratic integrity, highlighting the need for frameworks that address the socio-political dimensions of these freedoms.

Sunstein's (2021) insights into misinformation further complicate this relationship, particularly in an era where digital platforms amplify falsehoods rooted in religious or ideological zeal. The spread of misinformation not only distorts public discourse but also challenges policymakers to find solutions that balance countering deception with preserving fundamental freedoms. This issue is emblematic of the broader challenge of navigating the intersection of religion, speech, and democracy in a rapidly changing world.

Moving forward, it is imperative to adopt nuanced approaches that balance these freedoms, ensuring that neither is wielded to the detriment of the other. Policymakers must prioritise legal frameworks that reflect the complexities of multicultural societies, accounting for the power dynamics and cultural sensitivities that shape the exercise of these rights. Media literacy and education will also play a critical role in fostering informed public discourse, equipping individuals to navigate the often contentious intersections of religion and speech.

Moreover, fostering dialogue between religious communities, civil society, and governments is essential to developing solutions that respect diversity while upholding democratic values. In this regard, international cooperation and shared frameworks for addressing these challenges can provide a vital foundation. For example, lessons from legal systems that have successfully managed these tensions—such as Canada's balancing of multiculturalism with rights protections—can offer valuable insights for policymakers around the globe. Simultaneously, grassroots initiatives aimed at building trust between diverse communities are critical for fostering mutual understanding and reducing polarisation.

By embracing this multifaceted approach, societies can better safeguard both religious freedom and free speech, ensuring that these rights remain pillars of democracy rather than tools for division or oppression. A balanced and context-sensitive strategy is essential, one that protects the integrity of these freedoms while addressing their potential for exploitation in an increasingly interconnected and complex world.

Questions for Reflection

1. How can societies protect both religious freedom and free speech without allowing one to be used to suppress the other?

2. To what extent should legal systems tolerate offensive or controversial religious expression in the name of democratic values?
3. How do populist movements use religious rhetoric and free speech to shape public opinion and political power—and what are the consequences for minority communities?

Bibliography

Gey, S. G. 2000. When Is Religious Speech Not Free Speech. *University of Illinois Law Review*: 379.

Holzapfel, C. 2014. Can I Say That? How an International Blasphemy Law Pits the Freedom of Religion Against the Freedom of Speech. *Emory International Law Review* 28: 597.

Magarian, G. P. 2011. Religious Argument, Free Speech Theory, and Democratic Dynamism. *Notre Dame Law Review* 86: 119.

Mondal, A. A. 2016. Articles of Faith: Freedom of Expression and Religious Freedom in Contemporary Multiculture. *Islam and Christian-Muslim Relations* 27 (1): 3–24.

Morgan, B., ed. 2021. *Howl on Trial: The Battle for Free Expression*. City Lights Books.

Sunstein, C. R. 2021. *Liars: Falsehoods and Free Speech in an Age of Deception*. Oxford University Press.

Yilmaz, I., and N. Morieson. 2021. A Systematic Literature Review of Populism, Religion, and Emotions. *Religions* 12 (4): 272.

CHAPTER 8

Free Speech and Counter-Terrorism

Abstract This chapter critically examines the fraught relationship between free speech and counterterrorism in the context of contemporary UK and global security policy. Drawing on legal, philosophical, and technological perspectives, it explores how counter-terrorism frameworks often challenge, restrict, or redefine freedom of expression in the name of national security. Anchored in key academic contributions by Barak-Erez and Scharia, Donohue, Cram, and others, the chapter interrogates laws such as the UK's Terrorism Act 2006 and the Prevent strategy, raising concerns over vague legal language, disproportionate targeting of Muslim communities, and the criminalisation of dissent. The rise of "thought crimes," predictive policing, and algorithmic surveillance are explored as emerging threats to civil liberties, evoking dystopian parallels with speculative fiction and real-world examples like China's social credit system. The chapter also considers the evolving role of media and digital platforms in shaping public discourse around terrorism, often amplifying fear and legitimising overreaching state measures. Concepts such as moral panic, glorification, and self-censorship are used to analyse how counterterrorism responses can erode democratic accountability and marginalise dissenting voices. Particular attention is given to the impact on Muslim communities in the UK, where counterterrorism policies have fostered suspicion, alienation, and self-policing behaviours within public institutions such as universities. Ultimately, this chapter argues that the principles of proportionality and necessity must guide all counter-terrorism legislation, and

E.-J. Peatfield, *Free Speech in Contention*,
https://doi.org/10.1007/978-3-031-94109-2_8

that a deeper commitment to addressing the root causes of radicalisation—such as inequality, foreign policy grievances, and exclusion—is essential. Judicial oversight, media responsibility, and democratic dialogue are presented as vital tools in safeguarding the right to free speech in the face of expanding security regimes.

Keywords **Prevent Strategy**—UK policy aimed at identifying people at risk of radicalisation · **Terrorism Act 2006**—Criminalises acts like glorifying terrorism, raising speech concerns · **Thought Crime**—Criminalising ideas or beliefs before any action is taken · **Predictive Policing**—Using algorithms to identify individuals who might commit crimes · **Surveillance**—Monitoring individuals, often infringing on privacy and civil liberties · **Glorification of Terrorism**—Vague legal term used to penalise expressions of support · **Moral Panic**—Public fear exaggerated by media and politics, often leading to harsh policies · **Disproportionate Targeting**—When policies unfairly impact specific groups, especially Muslims

Introduction

This chapter explores the complex intersection of free speech and counter-terrorism, analysing how legal frameworks and policies attempt to balance the protection of individual freedoms with the imperative of national security. Drawing on key academic works, including Barak-Erez and Scharia (2011), Donohue (2005), and Cram (2019), the chapter examines how counter-terrorism measures impact freedom of expression and the broader implications for democracy. The discussion covers themes such as the regulation of extremist speech, the role of media, the concept of "thought crimes," and the effects on specific communities, particularly Muslims in the UK. The chapter critiques these measures through the lens of constitutional law and human rights, providing a nuanced understanding of the tensions between security and liberty.

The tension between free speech and counter-terrorism has become a defining issue in modern democracies. In an era of globalised communication and heightened concerns over terrorism, governments face significant challenges in balancing individual freedoms with the need to protect national security. While free speech is a cornerstone of democratic societies, the potential for its misuse to incite violence or support terrorism has led to the implementation of restrictive measures worldwide. Scholars have debated whether these measures strike the right balance or undermine the very freedoms they aim to protect.

Barak-Erez and Scharia (2011) argue that counter-terrorism laws often adopt a precautionary approach, restricting speech that may indirectly support terrorism. This precautionary logic raises critical questions about proportionality and the limits of constitutional law in addressing contemporary threats. Donohue (2005) similarly highlights the "future-oriented" nature of counter-terrorism policies, where governments act on potential risks rather than actual harm, often at the expense of free expression.

The Legal and Theoretical Framework

Freedom of Speech and Constitutional Law

Freedom of speech is enshrined in various legal instruments, including the Universal Declaration of Human Rights (Article 19) and the European Convention on Human Rights (Article 10). These provisions affirm the fundamental right to express opinions and access information without interference. However, this right is not absolute and can be lawfully restricted to protect national security, public order, health, morals, or the rights of others. Barak-Erez and Scharia (2011) highlight the inherent tension in determining the threshold at which speech becomes harmful enough to justify restriction. This balance is a complex and contentious issue, particularly in pluralistic democracies where conflicting values, such as free expression and societal harmony, often clash.

In the UK, the Human Rights Act 1998 incorporates the European Convention into domestic law, serving as a framework for resolving conflicts between free speech and other interests. Article 10(2) of the European Convention provides the basis for permissible limitations, emphasising that restrictions must be proportionate and necessary in a democratic society. Despite these safeguards, the UK's approach to free speech has drawn criticism for prioritising security concerns over expressive freedoms, particularly in the context of counter-terrorism.

Cram (2006) critiques the UK government's legislative approach, pointing to the Terrorism Act 2006 as a prime example. This Act criminalises the "glorification" of terrorism, a term that lacks precise definition and is therefore vulnerable to overreach. I would suggest that such provisions risk chilling legitimate political discourse, particularly among marginalised groups. For instance, political activists or journalists discussing controversial topics may face legal scrutiny, potentially undermining democratic debate.

Additionally, the Prevent strategy (2011) has continually faced criticism for its perceived impact on free speech. Barak-Erez and Scharia (2011) argue that measures targeting extremist narratives can unintentionally marginalise communities, fostering distrust in the legal system. My own research in (Peatfield, 2018) also showed a distinct distrust of Prevent and the driver of radicalisation identifies within it. Balancing the protection of public safety with the preservation of free expression remains an ongoing challenge, as courts, policymakers, and society continue to navigate this delicate terrain.

The Rise of Thought Crimes in Counter-Terrorism and Beyond

Galli (2013) examines the controversial concept of "thought crimes" in counter-terrorism, where individuals are prosecuted for their beliefs, expressions, or associations rather than concrete, harmful actions. This approach is rooted in the precautionary logic that extremist ideologies, if left unchecked, could escalate into acts of violence. However, while this rationale aims to pre-empt potential threats, it raises significant ethical and legal concerns about the criminalisation of dissent and the erosion of civil liberties. Galli argues that such measures blur the distinction between preventing terrorism and policing thought, threatening the principles of free expression and democratic debate.

At its core, the notion of a thought crime reflects a growing shift in legal frameworks from punishing acts to criminalising intent. This shift is particularly evident in counter-terrorism policies that prioritise the early detection and suppression of extremist ideologies before they manifest in violence. While the justification for this approach is rooted in national security concerns, it risks undermining core democratic values, such as freedom of thought, speech, and association. By broadening the scope of criminal liability to include ideological beliefs, governments set a dangerous precedent where individuals can be prosecuted for what they think rather than what they do.

This shift in legal paradigms evokes the dystopian premise of *Minority Report*, a 2002 film directed by Steven Spielberg and based on Philip K. Dick's short story. The film explores the concept of "precrime," where law enforcement uses precognitive technology to arrest individuals before they commit a crime. While *Minority Report* was initially seen as a far-fetched vision of the future, its parallels with modern counter-terrorism strategies are increasingly striking. Contemporary legal measures targeting extremist speech or glorification of terrorism mirror the film's premise, as they focus on intentions and potential risks rather than proven criminal acts.

Precrime in the Age of AI: The Rise of Predictive Policing

What once seemed like science fiction is fast becoming reality with the rise of artificial intelligence (AI) and predictive policing technologies. Governments and law enforcement agencies around the world are increasingly relying on AI-driven algorithms to assess the likelihood of criminal activity before it occurs. Predictive policing tools, powered by machine learning, analyse vast datasets—including social media activity, online searches, and even private communications—to flag individuals who may pose a future security risk.

The appeal of such technology is clear: if authorities can identify potential threats before they materialise, they could theoretically prevent acts of terrorism, mass shootings, or other forms of serious crime. However, the use of AI in law enforcement raises fundamental ethical and legal concerns. Unlike traditional criminal investigations, where guilt is established based on evidence of wrongdoing, predictive policing relies on statistical probabilities and behavioural patterns. This approach risks punishing individuals not for what they have done but for what they *might* do in future.

Moreover, AI-based systems are inherently flawed in their ability to accurately predict human behaviour. Algorithmic bias is a well-documented issue, with predictive policing tools disproportionately targeting marginalised communities, activists, and political dissidents. The fear is that such systems could be used to justify pre-emptive arrests, surveillance, or restrictions on individuals based on nothing more than a data-driven assumption of potential criminal intent. In this way, AI risks becoming the modern equivalent of *Minority Report's* "precogs," determining a person's guilt before any crime has even been committed.

The rise of thought crimes and predictive policing is intrinsically linked to the increasing surveillance capabilities of modern governments. In the wake of the 9/11 attacks, national security concerns led to the rapid expansion of state surveillance powers, with intelligence agencies granted unprecedented authority to monitor citizens. The revelations of whistle-blowers such as Edward Snowden exposed the extent to which governments engage in mass surveillance, collecting vast amounts of personal data without public consent.

The fear of a "Big Brother" society—where citizens are constantly watched, their conversations monitored, and their movements tracked—is no longer a paranoid conspiracy but a reality in many parts of the world. Advances in artificial intelligence, facial recognition, and data analytics have made it easier than ever for governments and corporations to monitor individuals on an unprecedented scale. In China, for instance, the social credit system uses AI-driven surveillance to assess citizens' behaviours, rewarding or punishing them based on their perceived trustworthiness. While such measures are often framed as necessary for maintaining security and social order, they raise serious concerns about privacy, autonomy, and human rights.

The UK's *Prevent* strategy, which aims to identify and intervene with individuals deemed at risk of radicalisation, exemplifies the dangers of state surveillance in counter-terrorism efforts. While proponents argue that *Prevent* helps to disrupt extremist recruitment, critics warn that it effectively polices thought and disproportionately targets Muslim communities. Reports have surfaced of students being referred to authorities for expressing political opinions, engaging in discussions about controversial topics, or even reading certain books. Such measures create an environment where individuals fear engaging in open debate, leading to self-censorship and the erosion of intellectual freedom.

The implications of policing thought are profound. By shifting the focus from actions to beliefs, governments risk eroding the very freedoms they seek to protect. This is particularly concerning in democratic societies, where the right to freedom of expression is a cornerstone of civil liberties. If individuals can be prosecuted for holding certain beliefs, the line between authoritarian control and legitimate law enforcement becomes increasingly blurred. One of the primary dangers of thought crime legislation is the potential for abuse. Laws criminalising extremist speech or "glorification" of terrorism are often vague and open to interpretation. This vagueness allows authorities to apply them selectively, targeting political dissidents, whistle-blowers, or activists under the guise of national security. In such cases, counter-terrorism measures become tools for suppressing dissent rather than preventing genuine threats.

A further concern is the impact on public trust in legal institutions. When governments are perceived as criminalising thought, it undermines confidence in the justice system and fosters resentment among affected communities. Instead of promoting genuine security, such measures can radicalise individuals by reinforcing a sense of persecution and injustice.

Striking a Balance: Security vs. Civil Liberties

While the need to prevent terrorism and violent extremism is undeniable, striking the right balance between security and civil liberties is essential. If counter-terrorism policies overreach, they risk violating the very freedoms they claim to defend. A more effective approach would focus on addressing the root causes of radicalisation—such as social inequality, political disenfranchisement, and lack of economic opportunities—rather than criminalising thought.

Policymakers must also ensure that AI-driven predictive policing is subject to rigorous oversight and ethical scrutiny. Transparency in algorithmic decision-making, clear legal safeguards, and mechanisms for challenging wrongful designations must be implemented to prevent abuses of power. Furthermore, greater accountability in government surveillance programmes is needed to protect citizens from unjustified intrusion into their private lives. In the broader context, societies must remain vigilant against the normalisation of thought crimes. If left unchecked, the logic behind pre-emptive justice could extend beyond counter-terrorism, seeping into other areas of governance. Already, similar arguments have been made for predictive policing in criminal justice, workplace monitoring, and even social media regulation. If the precedent is set that individuals can be punished for what they *might* do, rather than what they *have* done, the consequences for civil liberties could be far-reaching.

The rise of thought crimes, predictive policing, and mass surveillance represents one of the most pressing challenges of the digital age. While governments argue that such measures are necessary for security, they pose significant risks to freedom, democracy, and human rights. The fear of AI predicting behaviour, combined with the growing capabilities of state surveillance, raises urgent questions about the future of privacy and autonomy. As societies navigate these complex issues, the fundamental question remains: how much freedom are we willing to sacrifice in the name of security, and at what cost?

Counter-Terrorism and Media Regulation: The Role of Media

The media plays a pivotal role in shaping public perceptions of terrorism and government responses. The narratives presented by traditional and digital media significantly influence societal attitudes, policymaking, and even the perceived legitimacy of government actions. Cram (2006) underscores the centrality of media regulation in counter-terrorism strategies, particularly in the UK, where the government has sought to control the dissemination of extremist content as part of its broader security framework. The rationale behind this approach is to prevent the spread of radical ideologies that could incite violence or disrupt public order. However, this strategy often results in censorship and self-censorship, limiting the media's ability to hold power to account.

This dynamic is compounded by the concept of the self-fulfilling prophecy, where persistent media coverage of terrorism can reinforce fear and contribute to the very problems it seeks to address. For instance, by framing certain groups or ideologies as existential threats, media outlets may inadvertently validate government overreach, creating a cycle where public fear justifies restrictive measures. Such coverage not only marginalises communities but also risks normalising surveillance and censorship as acceptable tools of governance.

Stanley Cohen's seminal work on "folk devils" and "moral panic" (1972) provides a valuable lens for understanding how media narratives can amplify fear. Cohen argued that the media often constructs deviant groups as threats to societal values, fostering a moral panic that legitimises punitive responses. In the context of counter-terrorism, this pattern is evident in the portrayal of certain communities as breeding grounds for extremism. By sensationalising threats, the media can create an exaggerated sense of danger, prompting both public support for restrictive policies and self-policing behaviours among targeted groups. This not only erodes trust in democratic institutions but also perpetuates divisions within society.

Killion and Attorney (2019) explore how these issues are exacerbated by the rise of the internet and social media, which have become primary platforms for extremist propaganda, recruitment, and coordination. The global nature of these platforms complicates regulation, as content can easily cross authorities and evade national laws. Governments have increasingly pressured tech companies to remove extremist material, but this approach raises significant concerns about the privatisation of censorship. Critics warn that such measures place the responsibility for defining acceptable speech in the hands of corporations, which often lack the transparency and accountability necessary to navigate these ethical dilemmas.

Moreover, algorithms used by social media platforms to prioritise engagement often amplify sensationalist or fear-based content, further fuelling moral panics. This feedback loop contributes to public fear and supports the narrative that aggressive counter-terrorism measures are necessary, regardless of their impact on civil liberties. As Cohen (1972) warns, such cycles risk creating a society where fear and suspicion dominate public discourse, undermining the very freedoms that counter-terrorism policies aim to protect.

Ultimately, while regulating extremist content is essential, it is equally important to ensure that these efforts do not undermine the media's vital role in democratic accountability. As Cram (2006) and Killion and Attorney (2019) highlight, striking this balance remains one of the most pressing challenges in contemporary counter-terrorism strategies.

Neglected Issues in Media Regulation

Cram (2006) identifies several neglected issues in the regulation of media under counter-terrorism policies. One such issue is the overemphasis on suppressing extremist content while failing to develop and promote effective counter-narratives. Counter-narratives play a crucial role in challenging radical ideologies by providing alternative perspectives and addressing the underlying grievances that extremist groups exploit. Without these narratives, the media risks creating an informational vacuum that extremist ideologies can fill.

The regulation of online platforms, as Cram (2006) notes, often disproportionately affects marginalised communities, further entrenching existing social inequalities. For example, heightened surveillance of certain ethnic or religious groups perpetuates stereotypes and reinforces feelings of alienation, potentially increasing vulnerability to radicalisation. This dynamic underscores the need for a more nuanced approach that not only addresses security concerns but also protects democratic values such as equality, free expression, and social cohesion.

The media's portrayal of contentious geopolitical conflicts, such as the ongoing war in Gaza, further demonstrates its influence on public opinion and the shaping of global discussions. Coverage of this conflict has often been criticised for its polarised narratives. While Israel is frequently portrayed negatively, this representation has coincided with a documented increase in global antisemitism, as communities conflate criticisms of Israeli policy with hostility towards Jewish individuals. This complex interplay between media narratives and societal perceptions has significant implications. As Cohen (1972) suggests in his work on moral panics, such portrayals can escalate tensions, create folk devils, and exacerbate divisions within and between communities.

Moreover, the lack of balanced reporting on issues like Gaza exemplifies the dangers of focusing solely on suppressing extremist content without addressing bias or misinformation. This approach can deepen societal divides and stifle constructive dialogue, further complicating efforts to achieve security and justice.

Ultimately, Cram (2006) argues that counter-terrorism media regulation must go beyond censorship to include proactive efforts that foster understanding and inclusivity. Developing counter-narratives, promoting balanced reporting, and addressing systemic biases are critical to ensuring that counter-terrorism policies do not inadvertently undermine the democratic values they aim to protect.

Impact on Marginalised Communities; the Muslim Community in the UK

The text reads well overall, but I've adjusted it slightly for flow, clarity, and consistency while maintaining your original meaning:

Parker (2007) highlights the significant impact of the UK's counter-terrorism laws on the Muslim community, drawing attention to the disproportionate scrutiny and stigmatisation they face. Measures such as the Terrorism Act 2006 have been criticised for their focus on Muslim individuals and organisations, fostering a climate of fear and mistrust. My own work (Peatfield, 2018) criticised the Prevent strategy (2011) for singling out Muslims as the only religious group explicitly mentioned in the document. This disproportionate targeting has not only eroded social cohesion but also undermined the perceived legitimacy of counter-terrorism measures. Many in the Muslim community feel unjustly criminalised, leading to alienation and distrust in state institutions. My research examined the perceptions of Prevent (2011) among both Muslim and non-Muslim minority communities, revealing that the strategy was widely viewed negatively within these groups. These dynamics risk creating the very conditions that counter-terrorism policies aim to prevent by pushing individuals further to the margins of society, where extremist narratives may find resonance.

Scott-Baumann and Perfect (2021) provide further insight into the impact of counter-terrorism policies on the Muslim community, particularly in universities. They argue that initiatives such as the Prevent strategy, designed to identify and mitigate risks of radicalisation, have inadvertently created an environment of surveillance and silencing. Muslim students and academics, in particular, report feeling under constant scrutiny, with their speech and behaviour subject to interpretation as potential signs of radicalisation. This "chilling effect" on free expression undermines universities' role as spaces for open debate, critical thinking, and intellectual exploration.

The Prevent strategy has also been criticised for its broad and vague criteria for identifying radicalisation, which can lead to misinterpretation and overreach. For instance, expressing dissenting political views or engaging in discussions about controversial topics, such as foreign policy or religion, may be mischaracterised as indicators of extremism. This not only suppresses free expression but also discourages constructive dialogue that could challenge extremist ideologies and foster mutual understanding.

The impact of these policies extends beyond universities. In wider society, media portrayals of Muslims as potential threats have exacerbated stereotypes and fuelled Islamophobia. Stanley Cohen's (1972) concept of moral panic provides a useful framework for understanding this phenomenon. The portrayal of Muslims as "folk devils" in media narratives perpetuates fear and reinforces the perception that counter-terrorism policies are necessary, even when they disproportionately affect marginalised communities. This cycle of fear and surveillance perpetuates divisions and weakens efforts to build cohesive and inclusive communities.

Moreover, these policies have broader implications for democratic values. The targeting of a specific community under the guise of counter-terrorism undermines the principles of equality and justice, eroding trust in the legal system and democratic institutions. As Parker (2007) and Scott-Baumann and Perfect (2021) emphasise, addressing these issues requires a fundamental shift in how counter-terrorism policies are designed and implemented. Rather than fostering suspicion and division, these measures must prioritise engagement, inclusivity, and the protection of fundamental freedoms.

Advocacy of Violence and Sedition

Sorial (2013) addresses the criminalisation of speech advocating violence or sedition, a contentious yet common feature of counter-terrorism laws. These measures are often justified by the need to prevent harm and maintain public safety, particularly in an era of heightened security concerns. However, such laws frequently lack precise definitions of what constitutes advocacy of violence or sedition, leading to arbitrary and inconsistent enforcement. This ambiguity creates significant challenges in distinguishing between legitimate expressions of political dissent and unlawful incitement to violence.

For instance, public support for resistance movements in conflict zones or criticism of oppressive regimes may be misinterpreted as advocating violence, even when such expressions fall within the bounds of free speech. The lack of clarity in these laws not only risks criminalising individuals who pose no genuine threat but also suppresses political discourse and silences voices critical of the status quo. Sorial argues that this vagueness undermines the rule of law, as individuals cannot reasonably predict what speech may be deemed illegal, leading to uncertainty and self-censorship.

The impact of these laws is particularly pronounced for marginalised groups, who are more likely to be targeted and scrutinised under counter-terrorism frameworks. Communities already subjected to stereotypes and discrimination often find themselves disproportionately affected by these measures, exacerbating social inequalities and deepening mistrust in state institutions. Sorial highlights the importance of clear and narrowly tailored legislation to ensure that counter-terrorism efforts do not erode fundamental freedoms or disproportionately burden vulnerable populations. Without such safeguards, the criminalisation of ambiguous forms of speech risks becoming a tool of oppression rather than protection.

Extremism and the Internet

Killion and Attorney (2019) emphasise the dual-edged nature of the internet in the context of counter-terrorism. Online platforms have become a breeding ground for the rapid spread of extremist ideologies, enabling groups to disseminate their narratives to a global audience. These platforms are often used to recruit individuals, coordinate activities, and share propaganda. The internet's global nature and the ability to remain anonymous have made regulating online extremist speech particularly challenging, as content can easily cross authorities or reappear in different forms after being removed.

At the same time, the internet presents significant opportunities for counter-terrorism efforts. Governments and security agencies have increasingly relied on online monitoring to track extremist networks and identify individuals who may pose a threat. The use of advanced algorithms to detect and flag radical content has become a central tool in disrupting extremist activities. However, as Killion and Attorney (2019) highlight, these efforts often involve invasive surveillance and algorithmic censorship, which raise critical concerns about privacy, free expression, and the role of technology companies in enforcing counter-terrorism measures.

The reliance on algorithms to moderate content is particularly problematic. Automated systems often struggle to differentiate between harmful extremist speech and legitimate discussions of political or social issues, leading to the over-removal of content. For example, academic discussions about terrorism, journalistic reports, or even satire may be flagged as extremist material, creating a chilling effect on free expression. Furthermore, the privatisation of censorship, where technology companies are tasked with regulating content on their platforms, raises concerns about accountability and transparency. Killion and Attorney (2019) argue that such practices risk undermining democratic norms by concentrating significant power over speech in the hands of private entities.

Donohue (2005) critiques this reliance on technology as a solution to the complex issue of extremist speech, arguing that it often fails to address the root causes of radicalisation. Social and economic inequalities, political grievances, and a sense of marginalisation are key drivers of radicalisation, yet these underlying issues are rarely addressed in technologically driven counter-terrorism strategies. Instead, the focus on surveillance and censorship risks creating a surveillance state where civil liberties are sacrificed in the name of security.

This erosion of privacy and freedom can lead to public distrust in government institutions, particularly among communities already marginalised by counter-terrorism policies. Donohue (2005) warns that such approaches may ultimately be counterproductive, as they fail to tackle the conditions that make individuals susceptible to extremist ideologies. Addressing these root causes requires a more integrated approach, including social investment, education, and inclusive policies, rather than relying solely on technological measures to suppress extremist speech.

Ultimately, while technology plays a vital role in modern counter-terrorism, its use must be carefully balanced with the protection of civil liberties and democratic principles. As Killion and Attorney (2019) and Donohue (2005) emphasise, over-reliance on surveillance and algorithmic censorship risks deepening societal divisions and alienating the very communities whose cooperation is essential in combating extremism.

Proportionality and Necessity in Counter-Terrorism Measures

Barak-Erez and Scharia (2011) emphasise the importance of proportionality and necessity as fundamental principles in evaluating counter-terrorism measures, particularly those that impact free speech. Restrictions on expression must be narrowly tailored to address specific and demonstrable threats, rather than imposing broad, sweeping limitations that risk eroding democratic values. This approach is crucial in counter-terrorism contexts, where the stakes are high, and the potential for overreach is significant.

Proportionality ensures that measures taken to address threats are appropriate to the level of risk they pose. For example, criminalising speech that explicitly incites violence can be considered proportionate to the threat of terrorism, as such speech has a direct and demonstrable link to harmful actions. However, extending these restrictions to include vague terms like the "glorification" of terrorism, as seen in the UK's Terrorism Act 2006, risks going beyond what is necessary. Such broad terminology can lead to the suppression of legitimate political discourse or cultural expression, disproportionately impacting certain groups. Barak-Erez and Scharia (2011) warn that this lack of precision undermines trust in the legal system and weakens the legitimacy of counter-terrorism measures.

Necessity, contentiously, requires that any restriction on rights or freedoms be demonstrably required to achieve a legitimate aim. In the case of counter-terrorism, this often involves balancing public safety with the protection of fundamental freedoms. Measures that are unnecessarily restrictive or fail to consider less intrusive alternatives are unlikely to meet this standard. For instance, while surveillance may be necessary in specific, targeted cases to disrupt terrorist plots, blanket surveillance of entire communities lacks justification and infringes on privacy and freedom of expression without unambiguous evidence of effectiveness.

This principle is particularly relevant when counter-terrorism measures disproportionately target marginalised communities, such as Muslims under initiatives like the Prevent strategy in the UK. Peatfield (2018) argues that these policies often fail to meet the threshold of proportionality and necessity, as they rely on broad and ambiguous criteria that cast suspicion on entire groups rather than addressing specific threats. This not only undermines social cohesion but also risks alienating the very communities whose cooperation is essential for successful counter-terrorism efforts.

Moreover, the principle of necessity highlights the importance of evaluating whether counter-terrorism measures address the root causes of radicalisation or merely treat its symptoms. Donohue (2005) critiques the tendency to prioritise punitive measures over social and economic reforms that could mitigate the conditions fostering extremism. For instance, addressing grievances related to inequality, discrimination, or foreign policy could reduce the appeal of extremist narratives without the need for sweeping restrictions on expression.

Barak-Erez and Scharia (2011) caution that the failure to adhere to proportionality and necessity in counter-terrorism measures risks creating a climate of fear and repression. This can lead to self-censorship, where individuals avoid discussing controversial topics or expressing dissenting opinions out of fear of being surveyed or criminalised. Such outcomes are antithetical to the democratic values that counter-terrorism policies purport to protect. Ultimately, proportionality and necessity serve as critical safeguards against the misuse of counter-terrorism measures. By ensuring that restrictions on free speech are narrowly defined, evidence-based, and essential to achieving legitimate aims, governments can strike a balance between protecting public safety and preserving the freedoms that form the cornerstone of democratic societies.

The Role of Judicial Oversight in Counter-Terrorism Measures

Judicial oversight is a critical mechanism for ensuring that counter-terrorism measures do not infringe on fundamental rights. Parker (2007) emphasises the vital role that courts play in scrutinising the implementation of counter-terrorism laws, particularly in cases involving free speech. Judicial review acts as a safeguard against the overreach of executive power, ensuring that restrictions on expression are proportionate, necessary, and consistent with democratic principles. However, while this mechanism is essential, it is not without limitations.

Courts often defer to the government's assessment of security threats, especially in the context of national security. This deference can make it challenging to challenge or overturn restrictions on free expression, even when such measures are overly broad or vague. For instance, terms like "glorification" of terrorism, as outlined in the UK's Terrorism Act 2006, leave significant room for interpretation. Judicial decisions in these cases frequently rely on the government's framing of what constitutes a security risk, limiting the scope for meaningful oversight. Barak-Erez and Scharia (2011) argue that this reliance on governmental assessments risks undermining the independence of the judiciary and its role as a neutral arbiter of rights and freedoms.

The principle of proportionality, highlighted by Barak-Erez and Scharia (2011), should guide judicial oversight in these cases. Courts are tasked with assessing whether restrictions on free speech are narrowly tailored to address specific threats and whether less intrusive measures could achieve the same objective. However, the complexity of balancing national security with individual rights often results in decisions that prioritise security concerns, especially in high-stakes cases involving terrorism. This judicial tendency to err on the side of caution can perpetuate a climate of fear and suppress legitimate dissent.

Scott-Baumann and Perfect (2021) add that judicial oversight becomes even more challenging when counter-terrorism measures disproportionately affect marginalised groups. Policies such as the Prevent strategy, which has been criticised for targeting the Muslim community, often come under judicial review. However, the courts' deference to executive decision-making in security matters means that the structural biases embedded in such policies are rarely addressed. This can result in the perpetuation of discriminatory practices under the guise of counter-terrorism.

While judicial review remains a cornerstone of democratic accountability, Parker (2007) highlights the need for courts to adopt a more robust stance in safeguarding fundamental freedoms. Without such vigilance, there is a risk that counter-terrorism measures will continue to erode civil liberties and undermine public trust in democratic institutions. Strengthening judicial oversight through greater scrutiny of government claims and an emphasis on proportionality could ensure that security measures do not come at the expense of core democratic values.

Conclusion

The interplay between free speech and counter-terrorism, as explored in this chapter, reveals a deeply complex and contentious area of policy and legal frameworks. At its core, this dynamic reflects the ongoing struggle to balance the protection of individual freedoms with the imperative of national security in a world increasingly shaped by global communication, ideological conflicts, and rapid technological advancements. One of the critical findings highlighted in this chapter is the tendency of counter-terrorism measures to prioritise security over freedoms, often at the expense of democratic principles. Barak-Erez and Scharia's (2011) emphasis on proportionality and necessity underscores the importance of ensuring that restrictions on speech are narrowly tailored to address specific threats, rather than being overly broad and indiscriminate. However, as examined through examples like the UK's Terrorism Act 2006 and Prevent strategy 2011, these measures frequently fail to meet these standards. The ambiguity surrounding terms such as "glorification of terrorism" creates significant room for interpretation, leading to the suppression of legitimate political discourse and cultural expression.

The Prevent strategy, as critiqued by Parker (2007) and Peatfield (2018), further exemplifies the disproportionate targeting of marginalised communities, particularly Muslims in the UK. The identification of Muslims as the only religious group explicitly mentioned in Prevent has not only eroded social cohesion but has also led to distrust and alienation within these communities. My research has shown that the negative perceptions of Prevent among both Muslim and non-Muslim minorities highlight the failure of such measures to gain the trust of those most affected. Instead of addressing the root causes of radicalisation, such as inequality, marginalisation, and grievances related to foreign policy, these measures risk reinforcing the conditions that make individuals susceptible to extremist ideologies.

The concept of "thought crimes," as analysed by Galli (2013), illustrates the dangers of criminalising beliefs and expressions rather than focusing on concrete actions. Modern counter-terrorism measures, in their attempt to act on potential threats, often venture into the realm of pre-emptive justice, akin to the dystopian premise of *Minority Report*. This shift from actions to intentions raises profound ethical and legal questions, undermining the principles of free expression and democratic accountability. Such measures not only blur the line between policing and surveillance but also create a chilling effect, where individuals are deterred from engaging in political or religious discussions for fear of scrutiny.

The role of the media, as explored through the works of Cram (2006) and Cohen (1972), adds another dimension to this debate. Media narratives, particularly those shaped by moral panic, have a profound impact on public perceptions of terrorism and the legitimacy of government responses. Coverage that sensationalises threats and perpetuates stereotypes, such as those surrounding Muslims or the war in Gaza, amplifies fear and division, legitimising restrictive policies that disproportionately target marginalised communities.

The rise of the internet and social media has further complicated this landscape, as platforms become both vehicles for extremist propaganda and tools for surveillance and censorship. The privatisation of censorship by tech companies, as noted by Killion and Attorney (2019), raises critical concerns about accountability and the erosion of democratic norms.

Judicial oversight, as Parker (2007) argues, remains an essential mechanism for ensuring that counter-terrorism measures do not infringe upon fundamental rights. However, the tendency of courts to defer to government assessments of security threats often limits the effectiveness of this oversight. While the principle of proportionality should guide judicial review, its application is often inconsistent, particularly when measures disproportionately affect marginalised groups. Strengthening judicial oversight and prioritising transparency and accountability are necessary to prevent counter-terrorism measures from undermining the very freedoms they aim to protect. This chapter underscores the need for a more balanced and nuanced approach to counter-terrorism. As argued by Barak-Erez and Scharia (2011), restrictions on free speech must be both proportionate and necessary, addressing specific threats without eroding fundamental freedoms. Additionally, the importance of addressing the root causes of radicalisation, as emphasised by Donohue (2005), cannot be overstated. Social and economic reforms, inclusive policies, and the development of counter-narratives that challenge extremist ideologies are crucial components of any effective counter-terrorism strategy.

Ultimately, this chapter demonstrates that the tension between free speech and counter-terrorism is not just a legal or policy issue but a broader question about the values that underpin democratic societies. The erosion of civil liberties in the name of security risks creating a society defined by fear, division, and repression. To avoid this outcome, governments must adopt approaches that prioritise engagement, inclusivity, and the protection of fundamental rights, ensuring that the fight against terrorism does not come at the expense of the freedoms that define democracy.

Questions to Reflect On

1. To what extent can counterterrorism measures be justified in limiting free speech, and where should the line be drawn?
2. How do concepts such as "thought crime" and predictive policing challenge traditional understandings of justice and individual rights?
3. In what ways do media narratives around terrorism influence public support for policies that may undermine civil liberties?

Bibliography

Barak-Erez, D., and D. Scharia. 2011. Freedom of Speech, Support for Terrorism, and the Challenge of global Constitutional Law. *The Harvard National Security Journal* 2: 1.

Cohen, S. 1972. *Folk Devils and Moral Panics: The Creation of the Mods and Rockers*. Routledge.

Cram, I. 2006a. Regulating the Media: Some Neglected Freedom of Expression Issues in the United Kingdom's Counter-Terrorism Strategy. *Terrorism and Political Violence* 18 (2): 335–355.

Cram, I. 2006. *Terror and the War on Dissent: Freedom of Expression in the Age of Al-Qaeda*. Springer.

Cram, I., ed. 2019. *Extremism*. Free Speech and Counter-Terrorism Law and Policy: Routledge.

Donohue, L. K. 2005. Terrorist Speech and the Future of Free Expression. *Cardozo Law Review* 27: 233.

Galli, F., 2013. Freedom of Thought or 'Thought Crimes? Counter-Terrorism and Freedom of Expression. In *Counterterrorism, Human Rights, and the Rule of Law* (pp. 106–127). Cheltenham: Edward Elgar Publishing.

Killion, V. L., and L. Attorney. 2019. Terrorism, Violent Extremism, and the Internet: Free Speech Considerations. *Congressional Research Service* 6.

Parker, E. 2007. Implementation of the UK Terrorism Act 2006—The Relationship Between Counterterrorism Law, Free Speech, and the Muslim Community in the United Kingdom Versus the United States. *Emory International Law Review* 21: 711.

Peatfield, E. J. 2018. *Race and Radicalisation: Examining Perceptions of Counter-Radicalisation Policy Amongst Minority Groups in Liverpool 8 and 24*. United Kingdom: The University of Liverpool.

Scott-Baumann, A., and S. Perfect. 2021. *Freedom of Speech in Universities: Islam, Charities, and Counterterrorism*, 152. London: Taylor & Francis.

Sorial, S. 2013. *Sedition and the Advocacy of Violence: Free Speech and Counterterrorism*. London: Routledge.

CHAPTER 9

Free Speech and Democratic Societies Conclusions

Abstract This chapter synthesises the major themes explored throughout the book, reaffirming free speech as both a foundational right and a site of continual negotiation within democratic societies. It highlights the dual role of free expression as a vehicle for progress and a potential source of harm, depending on its application. The chapter revisits key debates—such as cancel culture, protest rights, gender pronouns, academic freedom, religious expression, and counterterrorism—emphasising the tensions between individual liberties and collective responsibilities. It calls for nuanced legal frameworks, inclusive public discourse, and institutional accountability to ensure that free speech supports rather than undermining democracy. Central to this vision is the need for empathy, dialogue, and critical education as tools to foster social cohesion and safeguard democratic values in an era of increasing polarisation and misinformation. Free speech must be continuously protected and re-evaluated to remain a force for justice, equity, and meaningful change.

Keyword **Balance of Rights**—The need to weigh free speech against harm, safety, and equality · **Democratic Resilience**—A society's ability to maintain freedom and justice amid challenges · **Empathy in Debate**—Valuing others' perspectives and experiences in public discourse · **Critical Education**—Teaching people to think analytically and challenge misinformation · **Institutional Accountability**—Ensuring organisations protect rights and promote fairness · **Polarisation**—The

E.-J. Peatfield, *Free Speech in Contention*,
https://doi.org/10.1007/978-3-031-94109-2_9

growing division in societies over political or cultural issues · **Social Cohesion**—Unity among diverse groups through dialogue and mutual respect · **Ongoing Negotiation**—Free speech must evolve with society's needs and values

Conclusion and Thoughts

Free speech, as explored in this chapter, is a cornerstone of democratic societies, intellectual progress, and social cohesion. However, its application is far from straightforward, as it operates at the intersection of competing values, societal norms, and legal frameworks. Understanding what free speech means—and where its limits lie—requires navigating the complex balance between protecting individual rights and safeguarding public interests. In a world marked by polarised debates and evolving societal norms, the balance between individual expression and collective interests is under greater scrutiny than ever before.

At its core, free speech embodies the right to express opinions, ideas, and beliefs without fear of censorship or retaliation. This right is essential for fostering dialogue, challenging entrenched power structures, and promoting social progress. Historically, free speech has served as a tool for advocating change, from civil rights movements to environmental justice campaigns. However, free speech is not an absolute right; it is shaped by legal, cultural, and contextual factors that determine when and how it may be restricted.

Ultimately, free speech is both a right and a responsibility. It empowers individuals to participate in democratic processes, challenge injustice, and contribute to societal progress. At the same time, it requires thoughtful stewardship to ensure it does not perpetuate harm or exacerbate inequalities. Striking the right balance between protecting free expression and addressing its potential risks demands ongoing dialogue, robust legal frameworks, and a commitment to inclusivity and justice. These themes underpin the discussions of cancel culture, the right to protest, identity politics, academic freedom, religious expression, and counter-terrorism explored in this chapter.

The rise of cancel culture has brought profound changes to public and academic discourse, presenting both opportunities and challenges for how societies manage free expression, accountability, and inclusivity. Cancel culture operates at the intersection of empowerment and suppression, reshaping the boundaries of acceptable speech in ways that spark intense debate.

From one perspective, cancel culture serves as a democratising force, amplifying marginalised voices and holding powerful individuals and institutions accountable for harmful rhetoric or actions. Movements such as #MeToo demonstrate how digital platforms can mobilise collective action and challenge entrenched power structures. By providing a mechanism for historically silenced communities to demand justice, cancel culture fosters social change and disrupts systemic inequalities.

Conversely, the unregulated and often punitive nature of cancel culture raises concerns about its impact on free expression, intellectual freedom, and constructive dialogue. Critics argue that cancel culture fosters a climate of fear, where individuals self-censor to avoid public backlash or professional consequences. Furthermore, the decentralised and unpredictable nature of cancel culture complicates its role in public discourse, often leading to disproportionate consequences and the erosion of trust in mechanisms of accountability. Navigating cancel culture requires a nuanced understanding of its dual nature. By fostering spaces for meaningful exchange and prioritising pathways for growth and redemption, societies can address the complexities of cancel culture while upholding democratic values of free expression and mutual respect.

The interplay between politics, protests, and public assembly underscores the enduring importance of the right to protest in a democratic society. Rooted in Article 11 of the European Convention on Human Rights (ECHR) and enshrined in UK law through the Human Rights Act 1998, the right to protest allows individuals and groups to express dissent, advocate for causes, and hold authorities accountable. Protests, as a form of collective free speech, embody the power of public expression but require careful legal and social navigation to preserve democratic principles.

Contemporary protest movements, such as Extinction Rebellion and Just Stop Oil, highlight significant challenges in maintaining this balance. Legislative responses, such as the Police, Crime, Sentencing and Courts Act 2022, have sought to address disruptions but have been criticised for their vagueness and potential overreach. Excessive restrictions or uneven enforcement risks undermining public trust in authorities and eroding the perceived legitimacy of the state.

Ultimately, safeguarding the right to protest requires a commitment to upholding democratic values while addressing legitimate concerns about public safety and societal order. By ensuring fairness, proportionality, and inclusivity in legal frameworks and policing practices, protests can remain a powerful and legitimate expression of public will.

The complexities surrounding gender pronouns underscore the broader cultural and societal shifts occurring in contemporary identity politics. On the one hand, the embrace of inclusive pronoun practices represents a significant milestone in the recognition and validation of diverse gender identities. On the other hand, controversies and challenges associated with pronoun usage reveal deep-seated tensions within societal structures, linguistic norms, and political ideologies.

For many, being recognised by their chosen pronouns is not just a matter of respect but a fundamental affirmation of their humanity. However, cultural resistance and the politicisation of pronouns have amplified ideological divides. Critics often frame the push for inclusivity as an infringement on free speech or a departure from linguistic traditions, highlighting the need to navigate these tensions with care. These debates reflect broader tensions over the boundaries of free expression and the responsibilities it entails.

The discourse on gender pronouns will undoubtedly continue to evolve, reflecting ongoing shifts in societal norms and values. By embracing the complexities of pronouns, societies can foster a nuanced understanding of identity and cultivate an environment that values diversity, respect, and empathy.

Academic free speech in the UK is at a critical juncture, shaped by a complex interplay of legal, cultural, and institutional factors. The principle of academic freedom is both a right and a responsibility, requiring careful navigation of competing values and priorities.

Recent years have seen increasing contestation of academic free speech due to societal pressures, debates over the limits of free expression, and the role of universities in addressing equity and inclusion. The tension between promoting open dialogue and maintaining inclusive environments is particularly pronounced. Additionally, cultural shifts, such as the rise of cancel culture and online activism, have created new dynamics for academic debate, where individuals may feel silenced by fear of public backlash.

To uphold academic freedom, universities, policymakers, and academics must collaborate to develop transparent institutional policies, foster respectful debate, and ensure robust support for those facing pressures to conform. By doing so, higher education can remain a space for rigorous inquiry, critical debate, and social progress.

The relationship between religious freedom and free speech is inherently complex, requiring careful navigation to uphold democratic values while respecting cultural and religious diversity. These two fundamental freedoms often intersect in ways that reflect broader social, political, and cultural dynamics.

While religious freedom is a cornerstone of democratic societies, it must not be used to justify discrimination or suppress dissenting views. Similarly, free speech should not be an unchecked license for hate speech, misinformation, or the erosion of social cohesion. Nuanced approaches that balance these freedoms are essential, ensuring that neither is wielded to the detriment of the other.

By fostering dialogue between religious communities, civil society, and governments, societies can better safeguard both religious freedom and free speech. This balanced approach ensures these rights remain pillars of democracy rather than tools for division or oppression.

The interplay between free speech and counter-terrorism reveals a deeply complex and contentious area of policy and legal frameworks. At its core, this dynamic reflects the ongoing struggle to balance individual freedoms with national security.

Counter-terrorism measures, such as the UK's Terrorism Act 2006 and Prevent strategy, often prioritise security over freedoms, sometimes at the expense of democratic principles. The disproportionate targeting of marginalised communities, particularly Muslims, erodes social cohesion and creates distrust. These measures risk reinforcing the conditions that make individuals susceptible to extremist ideologies rather than addressing their root causes.

To avoid undermining the freedoms that define democracy, governments must adopt approaches that prioritise engagement, inclusivity, and the protection of fundamental rights. Addressing the root causes of radicalisation through social and economic reforms, inclusive policies, and counter-narratives is essential for any effective counter-terrorism strategy.

Conclusion

Free speech remains one of the most vital and contested elements of democratic life. As this book has explored, its boundaries and applications intersect with some of the most pressing issues of our time, from cancel culture to counter-terrorism. Balancing the right to free expression with the responsibilities it entails requires vigilance, nuance, and an ongoing commitment to democratic values.

The evolving nature of free speech highlights the need for societies to remain adaptable, fostering environments where diverse voices can coexist while ensuring that these freedoms are not weaponised to harm others. As Peatfield (2018) asserts, this balance is central to democratic resilience, requiring a fine line between safeguarding liberties and preventing misuse. By embracing dialogue, promoting empathy, and supporting robust legal frameworks, societies can create spaces where free speech contributes to progress, equity, and understanding. This involves actively engaging with dissenting voices, ensuring that marginalised perspectives are not drowned out, and resisting the polarisation that often accompanies contentious debates.

The challenges and opportunities of free speech reflect broader struggles over power, justice, and inclusion. Addressing these challenges demands collective effort—from individuals, institutions, and governments alike. Education plays a pivotal role here, equipping people with the critical thinking skills needed to navigate misinformation, challenge oppressive narratives, and foster a culture of accountability. Institutions must lead by example, upholding the principles of transparency and inclusivity, while governments must craft policies that protect free speech without enabling harm.

At its best, free speech is a catalyst for positive change. It empowers individuals to hold the powerful accountable, amplifies the voices of the disenfranchised, and fosters innovation by enabling the exchange of diverse ideas. However, as Peatfield (2018) emphasises, this is only possible if free speech is ***underpinned by shared values of respect***, empathy, and fairness. In an increasingly interconnected and complex world, this balance is not only achievable but essential for democratic progress. Through collective action and a renewed commitment to democratic principles, societies can ensure that free speech remains a cornerstone of justice, equity, and transformative change.

CHAPTER 10

Recommendations

Abstract This chapter concludes the exploration of free speech in democratic societies and offers five key recommendations to strengthen and safeguard this foundational principle in the 21st century. It argues that free speech must be understood not as a fixed entitlement but as a dynamic and shared responsibility shaped by societal, technological, and cultural change. The recommendations highlight the need to foster open dialogue through education, strengthen legal protections while preventing abuse, promote empathy and inclusivity in public discourse, hold digital platforms accountable, and prioritise collective responsibility across individuals, institutions, and governments. Together, these strategies seek to balance liberty with accountability, ensuring that free speech functions as a cornerstone of democratic resilience, justice, and transformative social progress.

Keywords Free Speech · Democracy · Inclusivity · Critical Thinking · Legal Protections · Digital Platforms · Accountability · Public Discourse · Collective Responsibility · Misinformation · Polarisation · Human Rights

This chapter will recommend five key strategies to navigate the complexities of free speech in contemporary society. These recommendations underscore the importance of viewing free speech not as a static right

E.-J. Peatfield, *Free Speech in Contention*,
https://doi.org/10.1007/978-3-031-94109-2_10

but as a dynamic principle that evolves with societal, technological, and cultural changes. By fostering education, inclusivity, accountability, and robust legal protections, societies can build a balanced and equitable framework for free expression that upholds **individual** freedoms while promoting **collective** well-being.

The strategies will emphasise the need for education to equip citizens with critical thinking skills, fostering inclusivity to ensure marginalised voices are heard, and promoting empathy in public discourse. They will also address the necessity of holding digital platforms accountable in the era of misinformation and polarisation and the importance of crafting and maintaining adaptable legal protections to safeguard free speech while preventing harm. Together, these strategies highlight the shared responsibility of individuals, institutions, and governments to sustain free speech as a cornerstone of democracy, justice, and transformative social progress.

Foster Open Dialogue Through Education

Education is a critical tool for promoting free speech in a way that builds understanding, mutual respect, and inclusivity. Schools, universities, and public institutions play a pivotal role in embedding the values of open dialogue and critical inquiry. By prioritising teaching critical thinking, media literacy, and the importance of respectful discussion, educational institutions can equip individuals to engage in constructive conversations, challenge misinformation, and navigate the responsibilities tied to free expression. As Peatfield (2018) argues, education has the power to cultivate spaces where diverse ideas can coexist without fear or hostility, laying the foundation for meaningful democratic engagement.

In the English education system, fostering dialogue has been encouraged through initiatives such as the *Prevent Duty* guidance, which emphasises the importance of creating “safe spaces” for debates within schools and colleges to reduce the risk of extremist narratives while protecting free speech. Similarly, universities in the UK are tasked with promoting free expression under the Higher Education (Freedom of Speech) Act 2023, which seeks to ensure academic institutions remain places of intellectual diversity and open discourse (UK Parliament 2023a). These frameworks highlight the need for balance—educators must navigate the tension between encouraging free expression and preventing harm or intimidation.

Moreover, embedding dialogical practices, such as Socratic questioning, debating clubs, and interdisciplinary discussions, can foster a culture of intellectual curiosity and engagement. Studies suggest that these methods improve students' ability to think critically and empathise with opposing viewpoints, thereby reducing polarisation, and enhancing civic participation (SEN Policy Research Forum 2021). By incorporating such methods, schools and universities can nurture informed citizens capable of making reasoned arguments while respecting the diverse experiences and perspectives of others.

Ultimately, education must prepare individuals to exercise their rights to free speech responsibly, both online and offline. This involves equipping young people with the tools to discern truth from misinformation, critically evaluate the ethics of their speech, and engage in debates with empathy and respect. As I have tried to highlight, fostering open dialogue within educational settings is a cornerstone of ensuring that free speech serves as a force for democratic resilience and social progress.

Strengthen Legal Protections While Preventing Abuse

Robust legal frameworks are essential to protect free speech while addressing its potential misuse, ensuring that individuals can express themselves without fear of retribution. Legal protections must balance the right to free expression with safeguards against harmful behaviours, such as hate speech, incitement to violence, and defamation. As Peatfield (2018) notes, maintaining this balance is crucial for preserving the integrity of democratic discourse while protecting vulnerable individuals and communities from harm.

In the UK, legislation such as the *Human Rights Act 1998* enshrines the right to freedom of expression under Article 10 but also recognises that this right can be restricted when necessary to protect national security, public safety, or the rights of others. Similarly, the *Public Order Act 1986* criminalises hate speech and incitement to violence, reinforcing the principle that free speech should not be weaponised to harm or intimidate. These frameworks illustrate the need for nuanced legislation that evolves alongside societal and technological changes. For example, the rise of digital platforms and globalised communication has introduced new challenges, such as cyberbullying, online harassment, and the proliferation of misinformation. Recent efforts, such as the UK's *Online Safety Bill*, aim to address these issues by holding tech companies accountable for harmful content while preserving lawful free expression (UK Parliament 2023a).

Regular reviews of such laws are necessary to ensure their relevance in addressing emerging challenges while avoiding overreach. For instance, legislation must carefully distinguish between protecting freedom of speech and inadvertently enabling censorship. This requires transparency in legal processes and clear definitions of terms like "harmful content" to prevent misuse of the law as a tool for silencing dissent. Public consultation and engagement with legal experts, civil society groups, and technology platforms are essential to creating frameworks that balance liberty with harm prevention.

Ultimately, legal protections for free speech must remain adaptable and grounded in principles of equity and justice. As Peatfield (2018) emphasises, laws alone are not enough; they must be supported by broader societal efforts, including education and advocacy, to create a culture where free speech is both protected and responsibly exercised. By ensuring that legal frameworks are fit for purpose in an increasingly interconnected and polarised world, societies can safeguard free expression as a cornerstone of democratic life.

Promote Empathy and Inclusivity in Public Discourse

A healthy free speech environment thrives on empathy and inclusivity, both of which are essential for fostering constructive dialogue and reducing polarisation. Governments, organisations, and media platforms should actively encourage diverse voices to participate in debates, with particular attention to amplifying marginalised and underrepresented groups. This approach ensures that public discourse reflects the full spectrum of society, making it more representative and equitable. As Peatfield (2018) emphasises, inclusivity in free speech is not just a moral imperative but a practical necessity for building resilient democracies.

Governments can play a leading role by promoting initiatives such as public forums, citizen assemblies, and community outreach programmes designed to engage individuals from all occupations. For example, citizen assemblies, such as those convened for deliberating on climate change policy in the UK, have demonstrated the potential for diverse groups to reach common ground through structured and empathetic dialogue

(OECD 2020). Media platforms and organisations should also take responsibility for ensuring inclusivity by creating opportunities for under-represented voices to be heard, whether through dedicated spaces for minority opinions or by addressing structural barriers that prevent participation.

At the community level, outreach programmes can bring together people with different perspectives to foster mutual understanding and break down ideological divides. Initiatives like the *Big Lunch*, a UK-based community project, demonstrate how grassroots efforts can create opportunities for meaningful conversations and strengthen social cohesion (Eden Project 2021). These initiatives promote inclusivity by emphasising commonalities over differences, making it easier to engage in empathetic dialogue.

However, promoting inclusivity also requires addressing systemic inequalities that limit participation in public discourse. This includes tackling barriers such as unequal access to education, digital infrastructure, and resources for marginalised communities. Media platforms, in particular, must actively combat echo chambers and algorithmic biases that can distort debates and marginalise certain voices. The UK government's *Integrated Communities Strategy* provides a useful framework for fostering inclusivity by supporting local projects aimed at bridging cultural divides and promoting shared values (UK Government 2019).

Ultimately, inclusive public discourse creates opportunities for dialogue that is constructive, empathetic, and representative of diverse viewpoints. As Peatfield (2018) notes, empathy is a critical component of free speech that enables societies to bridge divides and work towards common goals. By investing in initiatives that foster empathy and inclusion, governments, organisations, and media platforms can ensure that free speech remains a powerful tool for building understanding, reducing polarisation, and promoting democratic resilience.

Hold Digital Platforms Accountable

The digital age has significantly amplified the reach of free speech, presenting both opportunities and challenges. While the internet facilitates rapid information dissemination and diverse perspectives, it also enables the spread of misinformation, the formation of echo chambers, and the prevalence of online harassment. Recent developments underscore the complexities involved in moderating online content to protect freedom of expression while minimising harm.

In January 2025, Meta Platforms announced significant changes to its content moderation policies, including the cessation of third-party fact-checking and a shift towards user-driven "Community Notes." This move has raised concerns among advocacy groups, such as the Molly Rose Foundation, which fears that reduced oversight could lead to the proliferation of harmful content, particularly related to self-harm and suicide. The foundation has called upon the UK's Office of Communications (Ofcom) to implement stringent measures to protect vulnerable users. These policy changes reflect a broader trend among social media companies towards reducing content moderation efforts. Platforms like X (formerly Twitter) and YouTube have also relaxed certain content restrictions, citing a desire to promote free expression and reduce operational costs. However, critics argue that these moves may lead to increased dissemination of hate speech and misinformation, potentially undermining public trust, and safety.

To navigate these challenges, it is imperative for tech companies and social media platforms to adopt transparent content moderation policies that balance the protection of free speech with the need to prevent harm. Implementing user accountability measures and ensuring algorithmic fairness are crucial steps in this process. Moreover, collaboration with governments and civil society organisations can help develop comprehensive strategies to address the complex issues arising in the digital landscape.

The European Union's Digital Services Act (DSA) serves as a pertinent example of regulatory efforts to create a safer online environment. The DSA imposes obligations on online platforms to manage illegal content, enhance transparency in content moderation decisions, and assess systemic risks associated with their services. By enforcing such regulations, the EU aims to hold platforms accountable while safeguarding users' fundamental rights, including freedom of expression.

In the UK, the Online Safety Act 2023 introduces new duties for social media companies and search services, making them more responsible for their users' safety. The Act mandates the implementation of systems and processes to reduce risks associated with illegal activity and requires the removal of illegal content when it appears. While the digital age offers unprecedented opportunities for free expression, it also necessitates a careful balance between protecting this freedom and mitigating associated harms. Tech companies, policymakers, and civil society must work collaboratively to establish frameworks that uphold free speech while ensuring the safety and well-being of all users.

Prioritise Collective Responsibility for Free Speech

Free speech is not only a fundamental right but also a shared responsibility that requires the active participation of individuals, institutions, and governments. It is essential to recognise that the exercise of free speech comes with ethical obligations. Individuals must practice self-awareness and accountability in their expressions, ensuring that their words contribute to constructive dialogue, build understanding, and avoid harm. This includes taking responsibility for combating the spread of misinformation, engaging respectfully with opposing viewpoints, and fostering an environment where diverse perspectives can coexist.

Institutions, particularly in journalism, education, and the arts, have a pivotal role to play in upholding the principles of free speech. In journalism, truth-seeking and responsible reporting must take precedence, ensuring that information disseminated to the public is accurate, balanced, and fair. In academia, institutions should model best practices in open inquiry by promoting academic freedom and creating spaces for rigorous debate and intellectual diversity. I have highlighted that institutions are central to sustaining free speech as a tool for justice and democratic resilience, acting as guardians of ethical discourse and innovation. As a lecturer and researcher, this is key to my own ability to work.

Governments must engage in policies that balance the right to free expression with harm prevention. This involves creating clear and transparent legal frameworks that protect free speech while addressing hate speech, incitement to violence, and other harmful behaviours. Governments should also work to uphold equality of access to free speech, ensuring that marginalised communities are not excluded from public discourse. Initiatives such as funding for community projects, civic education programmes, and support for independent media can foster greater inclusivity and empowerment. The responsibility for sustaining free speech extends beyond the national level to the global stage, where international cooperation is essential in addressing cross-border challenges, such as online censorship, digital surveillance, and the suppression of dissent in authoritarian regimes. Multilateral initiatives, such as those led by the United Nations, play a key role in advocating for universal principles of free expression while addressing the nuances of cultural and political contexts.

Ultimately, collective action and cooperation across these levels are essential to ensure that free speech serves as a foundation for justice, inclusion, and democratic progress. By working together, individuals, institutions, and governments can create an environment where free speech is not only protected but also used as a force for social good.

I ultimately suggest the free speech must be seen not as a static right but as a dynamic and shared responsibility—one that requires vigilance, empathy, and a commitment to fostering equity and understanding in an increasingly interconnected world.

Bibliography

Eden Project. 2021. *The Big Lunch: Bringing Communities Together* [Online]. Available at: https://www.edenprojectcommunities.com. Accessed 28 January 2025.

OECD. 2020. *Innovative Citizen Participation and New Democratic Institutions: Catching the Deliberative Wave*. Paris: OECD Publishing.

Peatfield, E. J. 2018. *Race and Radicalisation: Examining Perceptions of Counter-radicalisation Policy Amongst Minority Groups in Liverpool 8 and 24*. The University of Liverpool (United Kingdom).

SEN Policy Research Forum. 2021. *The Role of Education in Promoting Civic Engagement and Dialogue*. London: SEN Forum Publications.

UK Parliament. 2023a. *Higher Education (Freedom of Speech) Act 2023* [Online]. Available at https://www.legislation.gov.uk. Accessed 28 January 2025.

UK Parliament. 2023b. *Online Safety Bill* [Online]. Available at: https://www.legislation.gov.uk. Accessed 28 January 2025.

UK Government 1986. *Public Order Act 1986* [Online]. Available at: https://www.legislation.gov.uk. Accessed 28 January 2025.

UK Government. 1998. *Human Rights Act 1998* [Online]. Available at: https://www.legislation.gov.uk. Accessed 28 January 2025.

UK Government. 2019. *Integrated Communities Strategy* [Online]. Available at: https://www.gov.uk. Accessed 28 January 2025.

Correction to: Free Speech in Contention

Correction to:
E.-J. Peatfield, *Free Speech in Contention*,
https://doi.org/10.1007/978-3-031-94109-2

In the original version of this book, the author's name has been misspelled as "Elizbabeth" instead of the correct spelling "Elizabeth" which has now been corrected. The book has been updated with the change.

The updated version of this book can be found at
https://doi.org/10.1007/978-3-031-94109-2

E.-J. Peatfield, *Free Speech in Contention*,
https://doi.org/10.1007/978-3-031-94109-2_11

Index of Themes

Chapter 1: What Is Free Speech?

- The philosophical foundations of free speech
- Legal definitions and protections under human rights law
- The limits of speech in democratic societies
- Tensions between liberty, harm, and responsibility

Chapter 2: Cancel Culture and the Boundaries of Accountability

- The rise of cancel culture and digital activism
- Power, accountability, and marginalised voices
- The tension between social justice and free expression
- Public shaming, self-censorship, and due process

Chapter 3: Free Speech, Politics, Protests, and Public Assembly

- The legal right to protest under Article 11 ECHR
- Recent legislation affecting protest rights (e.g. Police, Crime, Sentencing and Courts Act 2022)
- Disruption vs. democratic dissent
- Policing, public order, and state power

E.-J. Peatfield, *Free Speech in Contention*,
https://doi.org/10.1007/978-3-031-94109-2

Chapter 4: Theories of Free Speech and Contemporary Controversies

- Classic liberal defences of free speech (Mill, Meiklejohn, Berlin, Popper)
- Modern challenges: identity politics, misinformation, and hate speech
- Contextualising harm and tolerance
- Philosophical vs. legal justifications

Chapter 5: The Complexities of Gender Pronouns in Identity Politics

- Gender pronouns as markers of identity and inclusion
- Resistance, backlash, and free speech debates
- Intersection of feminist and transgender discourses
- Linguistic innovation and cultural adaptation

Chapter 6: Academic Free Speech in Crisis?

- The mission of universities and freedom of inquiry
- The Higher Education (Freedom of Speech) Act 2023
- Cancel culture, student protest, and institutional responsibility
- Balancing intellectual freedom with inclusivity and equity

Chapter 7: Religion, Free Speech, and Social Cohesion

- The tension between religious freedom and freedom of expression
- Blasphemy, satire, and public morality
- Populism, identity politics, and emotional mobilisation
- Legal frameworks and pluralism in multicultural democracies

Chapter 8: Counterterrorism and the Policing of Speech

- The securitisation of expression under counterterrorism law
- Thought crimes, pre-crime, and predictive policing
- Surveillance, AI, and the erosion of civil liberties
- Impact on Muslim communities and public trust

Conclusion: Free Speech in a Polarised Age

- Free speech as a democratic cornerstone and a site of contest
- The need for proportionality, dialogue, and empathy
- Responsibilities alongside rights
- Free speech as a tool for justice, inclusion, and change

Bibliography

Amnesty International. 2022. *The Right to Protest Under Threat: Crackdowns in the UK*. London: Amnesty International. Available at: https://www.amnesty.org/en/documents/eur45/5598/2022/en/. Accessed 28 Jan. 2025.

Barak-Erez, D., and D. Scharia. 2011. Freedom of Speech, Support for Terrorism, and the Challenge of Global Constitutional Law. *Harv. Nat'l Sec. J.* 2: 1.

Barendt, E. 2005. *Freedom of Speech*, 2nd ed. Oxford: Oxford University Press.

Barnett, S. 2022. Regulating Big Tech: Balancing Safety and Free Speech. *Media, Culture & Society* 44 (3): 543–559. https://doi.org/10.1177/01634437211070025.

Benesch, S. 2014. *Dangerous Speech: A Proposal for Countering Online Hate Speech*. Washington, DC: World Policy Institute.

Bérubé, M., and J. Ruth. 2022. *It's Not Free Speech: Race, Democracy, and the Future of Academic Freedom*. JHU Press.

Bradshaw, S., H. Bailey, and P. N. Howard. 2021. Digital Misinformation and Harm in the Global South. *Journal of Information Technology & Politics* 18 (2): 162–178. https://doi.org/10.1080/19331681.2021.1910018.

Clark, M. D. 2020. *Cancel Culture: Accountability or Punishment?* https://www.researchgate.net/publication/342789456_Cancel_Culture_Accountability_or_Punishment. Accessed 16 Dec 2024.

Cram, I., and H. Fenwick. 2018. Protecting Free Speech and Academic Freedom in Universities.

Cohen, S. 1972. *Folk Devils and Moral Panics: The Creation of the Mods and Rockers*. Routledge.

E.-J. Peatfield, *Free Speech in Contention*,
https://doi.org/10.1007/978-3-031-94109-2

Cram, I. 2006a. Regulating the Media: Some Neglected Freedom of Expression Issues in the United Kingdom's Counter-Terrorism Strategy. *Terrorism and Political Violence* 18 (2): 335–355.

Cram, I. 2006. *Terror and the War on Dissent: Freedom of Expression in the Age of Al-Qaeda*. Springer.

Cram, I. ed., 2019. *Extremism, Free Speech and Counter-Terrorism Law and Policy*. Routledge.

Darr, B., and T. Kibbey. 2016. Pronouns and Thoughts on Neutrality: Gender Concerns in Modern Grammar. *Pursuit-the Journal of Undergraduate Research at the University of Tennessee* 7 (1): 10.

Della Porta, D., and M. Diani. 2006. *Social Movements: An Introduction*, 2nd ed. Oxford: Blackwell Publishing.

Dershowitz, A. (2020). Cancel Culture: The Latest Attack on Free Speech and Due Process. Simon and Schuster.

Donohue, L. K. 2005. Terrorist Speech and the Future of Free Expression. *Cardozo L. Rev.* 27: 233.

Department for Digital, Culture, Media & Sport. 2021. *Online Safety Bill: Impact Assessment*. Available at: https://www.gov.uk/government/publications/online-safety-bill. Accessed 17 June 2024.

Eden Project. 2021. *The Big Lunch: Bringing Communities Together*. [Online]. Available at: https://www.edenprojectcommunities.com. Accessed 28 Jan 2025.

Ewing, K. D. 2021. 'The Police, Crime, Sentencing and Courts Bill 2021: A Dangerous Authoritarian Turn?' *Public Law* (October): 1–16.

Flew, T., F. Martin, and N. Suzor. 2019. Internet Regulation as Media Policy: Rethinking the Question of Digital Communication Platform Governance. *Journal of Digital Media Policy* 2 (1): 1–22. https://doi.org/10.1386/jdmp.2.1.1_1.

Furedi, F. 2021. *Why Borders Matter: Why Humanity Must Relearn the Art of Drawing Boundaries*. London: Routledge.

Galli, F. 2013. Freedom Of Thought Or 'Thought Crimes? Counter-Terrorism and Freedom of Expression. In *Counterterrorism, Human Rights, and the Rule of Law*, 106–127. Edward Elgar Publishing.

Gey, S.G., 2000. When is Religious Speech Not Free Speech. *U. Ill. L. Rev.*, 379.

Gillespie, T. 2018. *Custodians of the Internet: Platforms, Content Moderation, and the Hidden Decisions that Shape Social Media*. New Haven: Yale University Press.

Global Action Plan. 2020 *Children's Safety Online: Report Findings*. Available at: https://globalactionplan.org.uk. Accessed 18 Dec 2024.

Harper's Magazine. (2020). A Letter on Justice and Open Debate. *Harper's Magazine*, 7 July. Available at: https://harpers.org/a-letter-on-justice-and-open-debate/. Accessed 17 June 2024.

Holzapfel, C. 2014. Can I Say that? How an International Blasphemy Law Pits the Freedom of Religion Against the Freedom of Speech. *Emory Int'l L. Rev.* 28: 597.

Honeycutt, N., S. T. Stevens, and E. Kaufmann. 2023. The Academic Mind in 2022: What Faculty Think About Free Expression and Academic Freedom on Campus.

Human Rights Act. 1998. c.42. Available at: https://www.legislation.gov.uk/ukpga/1998/42/contents. Accessed 6 Jan 2025.

Hodson, J. 2007. Women Write the Rights of Woman: The Sexual Politics of the Personal Pronoun in the 1790s. *Language and Literature* 16 (3): 281–304.

Joyce, P., and T. Bennett. 2022. The Police, Crime, Sentencing and Courts Act 2022: A Threat to Protest in the United Kingdom? *Policing and Society* 32 (4): 450–469.

Killion, V.L., and L. Attorney. 2019. Terrorism, Violent Extremism, and The Internet: Free Speech Considerations. Congressional Research Service, 6.

Lester, A., D. Pannick, and J. Herberg. 2019. *Blackstone's Guide to the Human Rights Act 1998*, 7th ed. Oxford: Oxford University Press.

Livingstone, S., M. Stoilova, and R. Nandagiri. 2020. Children's Data and Privacy Online: Growing up in a Digital Age. *Media Policy Brief* 23: 1–20.

Liberty. 2021. *Policing Protest: A Threat to Democracy*? London: Liberty. Available at: https://www.libertyhumanrights.org.uk/report/policing-protest-a-threat-to-democracy/. Accessed 29 Jan 2025.

Lukianoff, G., and J. Haidt. 2018. *The Coddling of the American Mind: How Good Intentions and Bad Ideas are Setting up a Generation for Failure*. New York: Penguin Press.

Matsuda, M. J. 2018. Words that Wound: Critical Race Theory, Assaultive Speech, and the First Amendment. *Critical Race Theory*, 2nd ed. Chicago: University of Chicago Press.

Magarian, G.P. 2011. Religious Argument, Free Speech Theory, and Democratic Dynamism. *Notre Dame L. Rev.* 86: 119.

Mondal, A. A. 2016. Articles of Faith: Freedom of Expression and Religious Freedom in Contemporary Multiculture. *Islam and Christian-Muslim Relations* 27 (1): 3–24.

Morgan, B. (ed.). 2021. *Howl on Trial: The Battle for Free Expression*. City Lights Books.

Mead, D. 2010. *The New Law of Peaceful Protest: Rights and Regulation in the Human Rights Act Era*. Oxford: Hart Publishing.

McGlashan, H., and K. Fitzpatrick. 2018. 'I Use any Pronouns, and I'm Questioning Everything Else': Transgender Youth and the Issue of Gender Pronouns. *Sex Education* 18 (3): 239–252.

Mendes, O. 2021. Gender-Neutral Pronouns: They are Here to Stay. *Seton Hall L. Rev.* 52: 317.

Ng, E. 2020. No Grand Pronouncements Here...: Reflections on Cancel Culture and Digital Media Participation. *Television & New Media* 21 (6): 621–627.

OECD. 2020. *Innovative Citizen Participation and New Democratic Institutions: Catching the Deliberative Wave*. Paris: OECD Publishing.

Oleksiyenko, A. V., and L. Jackson. 2021. Freedom of Speech, Freedom to Teach, Freedom to Learn: The Crisis of Higher Education in the Post-Truth Era. *Educational Philosophy and Theory* 53 (11): 1057–1062.

O'Neil, C. 2016. *Weapons of Math Destruction: How Big Data Increases Inequality and Threatens Democracy*. New York: Crown Publishing Group.

Oliver, D. 2022. Protest and the Law: New Developments in the UK. *Legal Studies* 42 (3): 457–478. https://doi.org/10.1017/S026138752200020X.

Parker, E. 2007. Implementation of the UK Terrorism Act 2006-the Relationship Between Counterterrorism Law, Free Speech, and the Muslim Community in the United Kingdom Versus the United States. *Emory Int'l L. Rev.* 21: 711.

Peatfield, E.J. 2018. *Race and Radicalisation: Examining Perceptions of Counter-Radicalisation Policy Amongst Minority Groups in Liverpool 8 and 24*. United Kingdom: The University of Liverpool.

Police, Crime, Sentencing and Courts Act 2022. Available at: https://www.legislation.gov.uk/ukpga/2022/32/enacted. Accessed 5 Jan 2025.

Pew Research Center. 2021. Americans and 'Cancel Culture': Where Some See Calls for Accountability, others See Censorship, Punishment.

Price, C. 2019. Women's Spaces, Women's Rights: Feminism and the Transgender Rights Movement. *Marq. L. Rev.* 103: 1509.

Rowling, J.K. (2020) 'J.K. Rowling Writes about her Reasons for Speaking out on Sex and Gender Issues'. *jkrowling.com*. Available at: https://www.jkrowling.com. Accessed: 17 June 2024.

Schmid, A. P. 2013. Radicalisation, De-Radicalisation, Counter-Radicalisation: A Conceptual Discussion and Literature Review. *ICCT Research Paper* 1 (1): 1–39.

Scott-Baumann, A., and S. Perfect. 2021. *Freedom of Speech in Universities: Islam, Charities, and Counterterrorism*, 152. Taylor & Francis.

Sorial, S. 2013. *Sedition and the Advocacy of Violence: Free Speech and Counterterrorism*. Routledge.

Siewierska, A., 2013. Gender Distinctions in Independent Personal Pronouns. *The World Atlas of Language Structures Online*. The World Atlas of Language Structures Online.

Simons, G. 2022. Extinction Rebellion and the Right to Protest: Disruptive Activism in a Democratic Society. *Social Movement Studies* 21 (4): 512–530. https://doi.org/10.1080/14742837.2022.2034341.

Simpson, R. M. 2020. The Relation Between Academic Freedom and Free Speech. *Ethics* 130 (3): 287–319.

Smith, E. 2019. Legitimacy and the Policing of Protest: The Role of Discretion in Undermining Public Trust. *British Journal of Criminology* 59 (5): 1237–1255.

Sunstein, C.R. 2021. *Liars: Falsehoods and Free Speech in an Age of Deception.* Oxford University Press.

Turk, J.L. ed. 2014. *Academic Freedom in Conflict: The Struggle Over Free Speech Rights in the University.* James Lorimer & Company.

UN Human Rights Council 2021. *Report of the Special Rapporteur on the Rights to Freedom of Peaceful Assembly and of Association.* A/HRC/47/25. Available at: https://undocs.org/A/HRC/47/25. Accessed 29 Jan 2025.

UK Parliament (2023). *Online Safety Bill.* [Online]. Available at: https://www.legislation.gov.uk. Accessed 28 Jan 2025.

UK Government (1998). *Human Rights Act 1998.* [Online]. Available at: https://www.legislation.gov.uk. Accessed 28 Jan 2025.

UK Government (1986). *Public Order Act 1986.* [Online]. Available at: https://www.legislation.gov.uk. Accessed 28 Jan 2025.

UK Government (2019). *Integrated Communities Strategy.* [Online]. Available at: https://www.gov.uk. Accessed 28 Jan 2025.

Walker, C. 2019. Counter-Terrorism, Free Speech and the Right to Protest in the UK. *European Human Rights Law Review* 1: 35–51.

Ward, S. 2014. *Ethics and the Media: An Introduction.* Cambridge: Cambridge University Press.

Yilmaz, I., and N. Morieson. 2021. A Systematic Literature Review of Populism, Religion, and Emotions. *Religions* 12 (4): 272.

Zietlow, R. E. 2000. Beyond the Pronoun: Toward an Anti-Subordinating Method of Process. *Tex. J. Women & L.* 10: 1.

FSC
www.fsc.org
MIX
Papier | Fördert gute Waldnutzung
FSC® C083411

Kolibri 360 GmbH
Ferdinand-Jühlke-Straße 7
99095 Erfurt, Deutschland
produktsicherheit@kolibri360.de